300 TO 500
EVERYDAY!

GARY TAAFFE

How I get 300 to 500 hits on my Amazon Book Page EVERYDAY!

STAMPEDE

BUNYA PUBLISHING.com

Bunya Publishing books may be purchased for educational, business, or sales promotional use. For information, please write to: Special Markets Dept, Bunya Publishing, P.O. Box 10, Forster, NSW, 2428, Australia.

Image of shoppers courtesy of Press Association

Cover artwork by Gary Taaffe Copyright © Gary Taaffe 2014

ISBN: 978-0-9923796-3-6

Edition: v21.7.14

B **BUNYA**
PUBLISHING.com

Contents

Introduction

What you're about to read will go against most of what you've ever read about social media. I struggled with it for a long time as I know many of you have too, but I figured out why that is. I figured out how to simplify the process and at the same time,- make it work for me.

I've been self-publishing my own books for years now. As of this moment I've got eight fictional adventure stories published in my Urban Hunters series. I did all the supposedly correct things to promote my books with website, blog, social sites and a newsletter. I've listed my books everywhere that allowed me to and pleaded for reviews with anyone who'd listen. It's taken me years to set all this up. Truly! Years! I soaked up all the guru's advice like a sponge and did many of the things they suggested. Eventually I progressed through my apprenticeship stage and found my feet. I realised that the guru's list of what I should be doing was never going to end.

I like to do things a little differently because the process often reveals wonderful new discoveries. I've had plenty of failures and wasted lots of time in the process but I have had a few successes along the way. None of them though, have come even close to the massive success I've been experiencing lately.

STAMPEDE

News through the grapevine of social media revealed a simple solution to a complex problem I'd been struggling with for quite some time. Finally, I had a one click solution for sending customers direct to my Amazon Book Pages, and the missing link to a potentially awesome marketing system that I'd been working on.

I applied this new one click solution to my automated marketing system and all of a sudden, I was getting immediate mind–blowing results. It was like a stampede of customers banging on my door 24 hours a day, 7 days a week. I began thinking of it as a stampede and referring to my system that way when I explained it to my wife. And so the name has stuck— Stampede!

If you follow the procedures in this book, you'll be discovered by masses of readers who would never normally hear about you. In fact, you'll shine above all the best sellers and continue to do so day in day out for years to come.

Discoverability is the new buzz word for authors and Stampede cuts through the mystery of it like a buzz saw. And what's even better is a complete and utter newbie can do it, without a website, a blog, a newsletter and years of nurturing a social network. Actually, my advice to a newbie is to forget all about those time sapping things for now and get Stampede up and running first and foremost.

Nothing I have ever done comes even close to the success of this system and I've got over 10,000 Twitter followers. This system doesn't need any of them.

That was just a couple of weeks ago. I started at my desk this morning with an idea of how I could tweak my strategy but in the process, I began writing, I'm up to here. You're here too because you've decided to buy this book that I didn't know I was going to write, let alone have the time to write. I'm about to run you through the whole process and you're about to see the same results that I've been seeing.

Here we go.

Authors are Accidentally Creating Racist Book Links

W hen you list your book or product with Amazon.com and they create your book page, your book is automatically fed out to all the Amazon countries who also create a book page for you: Amazon America, India, England, Denmark, France, Spain, Italy, Japan, Brazil, Canada, Mexico and Australia. Each country creates a book page for you with its own unique web address. So the dilemma for authors has been which country do you send your customers to? Or which URL do you use in your marketing?

Authors typically send customers to Amazon.com, but a French customer doesn't want to be sent to Amazon in America when they can get the same book from Amazon in France.

The French customer would have to click out of Amazon.com, type Amazon France into their Google search bar, read through the Google list presented, click on Amazon France, type the name of your book into the Amazon France search bar, if they can remember the name of your book, read through the books presented, click on yours and finally, get to your book in Amazon France. Phew.

But hang on, customers drop off at an estimated 50% per click so they're never going to get that far anyway. You may have done the impossible by getting 100 customers to click on your book link but you'd be lucky if 5 reached your buy now button.

Stampede will get them to the buy now button in their own country with just one click.

How to Create Non–Racist Book Links

Send customers direct to the buy now button in their own country by creating a Universal Book Link.

If a person in France clicks your Universal Book Link, they'll be sent to your book page in Amazon France. If a person in Australia clicked that very same link, they'd be sent to your book in Amazon Australia.

The Australian customer doesn't have to freight the book all the way from America, and the book is in their hands within a day or two instead of a week or two. In the time it would have taken for the book to arrive from America, they could have bought and read some of your other books.

BookLinker.net is a site that allows you to create these Universal Book Links. **Update Oct 2014:** I now use **GeoRiot**, they're much more professional and are feature rich. The principles are the same as in the following BookLinker guide.

Here's my link in action.

This is the Amazon.com URL to one of my eBooks:

http://www.amazon.com/Four-Small-Stones-Urban-Hunters-ebook/dp/B005FG6486/

And here it is transformed into a BookLinker Universal Link:

http://getbook.at/FSSe

This is my new GeoRiot link: **http://geni.us/1N7u.**

Here's the screenshot of BookLinker counting how many times the link has been clicked.

3,752 hits! That's 469 hits per day since I set up Stampede just eight days ago. How good is that!

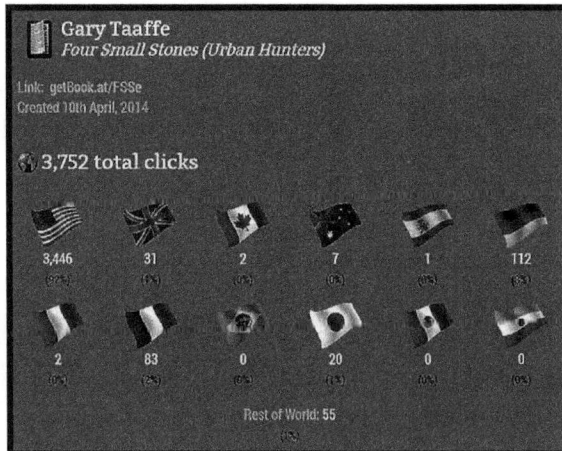

And here's that same link as I send this book to the editors. Going well isn't it?

Let's create your link.

Go to BookLinker and set up your free account with a username and password.

Make a decision about which format of your book you want to send customers to: eBook, Print book or perhaps Audio book etc.

Ebooks are the most popular format for my customers so I choose that for most of my marketing. If you're marketing specifically to audio book buyers then create a Universal Link for that. BookLinker allows you to create as many links as you like.

Highlight the Amazon.com URL for your book's page through your browser's address bar. Here's mine:

http://www.amazon.com/Four-Small-Stones-Urban-Hunters-ebook/dp/B005FG6486/ref=la_B005G035V0_1_1_title_1_kin?s=books&ie=UTF8&qid=1399857571&sr=1-1

It's a lot longer than the URL I showed you before isn't it? All that gobbledygook after your ASIN number is tracking information for Amazon and is not necessary so delete it to get this:

http://www.amazon.com/Four-Small-Stones-Urban-Hunters-ebook/dp/B005FG6486/

Enter it into the little window and hit "Create universal link".

A new window gives you the following choices:

- mybook.to

- viewbook.at

- getbook.at

You're trying to *sell* your book, not just *promote* it or yourself as an author. Getbook.at is a call to action to buy your book so that is the obvious choice for sales if you ask me. Even if a person is just curious and clicks the link to your book's page without any intention of buying it, that subliminal message of getbook.at rolling around the back of their head just might be enough to encourage them to push that buy now button.

After that, you have the option of adding your own text. I shorten my book's title and the format identifier. My Four Small Stones eBook becomes FSSe, to keep the link as short as possible. I'll be showing you how to use these links on Twitter and Twitter only allows you 140 characters per tweet, so keep it short.

NOTE: I create other links to the same book but with slightly different identifiers. I do that to use them on my website so I can see how many people are coming to my Amazon Book Page from my website.

Once you check the little box agreeing to BookLinker's terms, click the create link button and your link will be ready for you to copy and paste into your list of links. I'm forever copying and pasting links to my books, my website, my blog and a myriad of other things so I list them all in a Microsoft Excel spreadsheet which I find works really well.

BEWARE THE AMAZON ERROR MESSAGE

Print books and Audio books are not available through every country's Amazon. For example, if someone from France clicked on your Universal Book Link for your print book and Amazon France didn't stock your print book, an Amazon error message would pop up.

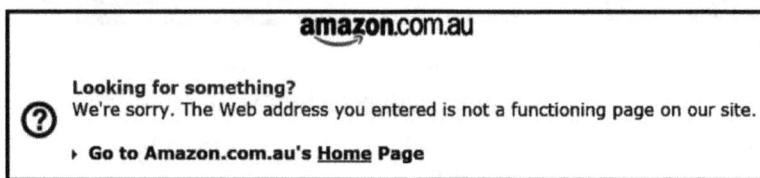

amazon.com.au

Looking for something?

We're sorry. The Web address you entered is not a functioning page on our site.

▸ **Go to Amazon.com.au's Home Page**

To counteract this problem, I add this message beside the link on my website: (Amazon webpage error message means it's not available in your country. Purchase direct from **Amazon USA** or use the "Add to Cart" button below to buy direct from **Bunya Publishing Australia.**

NOTE: BookLinker is part of my Stampede system but it's certainly not essential. Stampede will work no matter what product or business you are promoting.

Social Media
the Easy Way

Authors are introverts for the most part, and all this social networking stuff is extroverted. That's why you've been tearing your hair out trying to do it. Well the good news is you don't have to do it anymore if you don't want to because I've come up with this fantastic system that gets around all of it. Read on.

Social networking sites are buzzing with millions and millions of busy bees building their hives ever bigger. Lots of people on the constant lookout for something to chat about. Your job as an author, or as a business person, is to give them something to chat about, not to be the one doing all the chatting, unless you want to.

I think that's where the gurus have gotten it all wrong. Just because you're on or using social media doesn't mean you have to be the one being social. That's chatty Cathy's job and she's really good at it. Your job is to be really good at writing, to give chatty Cathy something to chat about. Does that make sense to you? Would you prefer to use social media that way? It *is* OK to *use* social media. That's what everyone else is doing anyway, including chatty Cathy. She's using it to be social, you're using it to market your book.

Companies market their wares all the time. Social networks are dependent upon it for growth and income, and Cathy understands that. Actually, she doesn't mind because social sites are so clever these days that they know that Cathy likes high heel shoes so they put advertisements for high heels right where Cathy is going to see them. Your job is to do the same, without ever over doing it and being a pest.

Normally, to place your ad exactly where Cathy is going to be, you'd have to be friends with her, or else you'd have to pay for advertising. I'm going to show you how to do it for free, on a very, very large scale. But first I'm going to show you how I use social media in general.

Aside from Twitter, which I'll get to shortly, I do almost nothing on any of the social networking sites anymore. I pay nothing for advertising and yet I get truckloads of traffic to my Amazon Book Page. I use those social sites for the free marketing they provide to the millions of people who use them.

My Facebook Author page is simply there for Facebook people to find me if they want to do a Facebook search for me. Someone in LinkedIn will search for me there, and so on with the other sites. I go to all those sites and lock in my username, place an author image, bios, book images and blurbs and prominently place my Universal Links to my Amazon Book Pages.

If someone wants to chat with me on any of those sites, I'll be notified and I'll happily get back to them as soon as I can, often instantly, but I don't push for a chat anymore because I'm not there to be social. I focus on providing the information they need about my books and encouraging them to follow my links to my buy now buttons. No messing about. No distractions. Straight to the point. Buy now.

That *is* what they want anyway. People don't want to spend half an hour getting to know the Nike guy, they want his shoes, that's all. It's the same with your book. Authors aren't the celebrities they used to be. You have a product that people want. Give it to them. Don't try to be their friend. If they like your book they'll follow you on Facebook and/or subscribe to your newsletter where you'll be able to offer them a great deal on your next book.

Gurus are telling people exactly the opposite. They're wrong. They're telling people to build a long term relationship in order to get sales down the track. That's all well and good but the way they tell you to do it is costing you a fortune, in time. They want you to be in constant communication with all these people, constantly entertaining so occasionally, ever so gently so as not to offend anyone, you can hit them up with a sale. It's too constant. It's costing you too much in time and besides, strangers don't want to be spending their precious time reading your desperate friend finding dribble, they want to be talking to their actual friends.

All that being said, I have become quite good friends with some fans and I love talking with them, but the point is that I *like* talking with them. I *like* spending time with them and they *like* talking with me. I *don't* like busting a gut *trying* to be friends with a very long list of total strangers. Fans contact me to tell me they like my books and friendships grow from there. The difference is that I'm not trying to be friends with them before they like my books, that's way too hard, the friendship comes later and when it does, it's genuine.

I did all the things the gurus told me to do by building a social network and writing a blog etc until I realised that their list of what I should be doing was never going to end. They had to keep coming up with things for me to do to keep their guru status. Hogwash!

I used to write a blog post and feed it out to all my social sites, or vice versa which took me ages and ages to do. I did all that over and over again once a week if not more. Those great Facebook posts I wrote would have to be rewritten to suit a blog post, and rewritten again for Twitter. Blah blah blah. On and on it went along with my precious writing time. And was I seeing results in sales from all that time? Not really. Sometimes I'd see spikes in sales but it was far from significant.

All I do now, other than Stampede, which works on AutoPilot in the background anyway, is write an excellent newsletter once a month. I post a link to it on all my social sites and copy and paste it as a blog post. That's it. That's all. Nothing else. It's so much easier and it's way more effective.

Only a small percentage of people on Facebook see my Facebook posts whereas everyone who subscribes to my newsletter gets it in their email inbox where they can choose to read it or not. Most do. And I know this because I use MailChimp which tells me who got my newsletter and if they opened it. It's fantastic and it saves me so much time. Subscribe to my newsletter through my Bunya Publishing website for a good example of how I do it. Unsubscribe anytime if you wish.

The other thing I do, other than Twitter which I'm still getting to, is I set up an excellent website for selling my books direct. It's a 100% royalty direct to my pocket and worth the effort. Check it out for another good example of what to do: **www.BunyaPublishing.com**

The only caveat to the website I'd suggest is if you only have one or two books for sale, I'd keep things super simple by going with the Amazon Select program which you're only eligible for if you sell through Amazon exclusively. Set up Stampede with your Universal Links sending masses of customers to your Amazon Book Page and spend your time writing your next book. Create a website when you have enough books to set up short term specials and sales and things like that. But for now, keep it simple.

Let me give you another reason why keeping it simple can be to your advantage.

Lets say you have a blog or a website filled to capacity will all manner of interesting and entertaining things to entice a customer to buy your book. Things like YouTube book trailers and videos of you reading excerpts and any number of other new fangled bells and whistles. Get rid of them all. They're distracting your customers from buying your book. Lead them directly to your buy now button. Do not pass go, do not let them collect a moment of entertainment, send them direct to your buy now button on Amazon where you can entertain the heck out of them after they've paid you for the entertainment.

It's the same with Google. If someone punches in your name and up pops ten listings, and one of them is their favourite social site, then that's where they're going to go. But they can't buy your book there so what's the point of sending them there? You want them to have one choice and one choice only— Amazon, where your buy now button is.

In the time it takes you to set up all those things, desperately trying to sell the book you've just written, you could have written another great book. Believe me, I've done it. I did all those things. Being an author is all about writing books, not being a social guru. Act professionally and pump out lots and lots of great books, not lots and lots of great Facebook posts. Use this Stampede system for your marketing and save yourself loads and loads of time for writing.

OK, let's get into Twitter because that's where all the magic happens.

No Social Following Needed at all

You don't need a Twitter following for Stampede to work, in fact you don't need any followers at all.

No strategy I've ever used has come even close to the sheer quantities of customers I'm sending to my door using Stampede. If I stopped everything else, it would hardly slow the Stampede down in the slightest. So if you're a newbie, for now, forget about setting up a blog, website, newsletter and Facebook or anything else for that matter, except for Twitter. Twitter is the cornerstone of my Stampede strategy and is essential.

Like the other social sites I mentioned earlier, Twitter is chock–a–block full of worker bees building traffic for you to tap into. Plus, there are external programs that allow you to do it on AutoPilot, on a very, very large scale. On top of all that, there are mechanisms within Twitter that allow you to put your message in front of the whole Twitter nation. You can't do that on Facebook— talk to *everyone* on Facebook. You can only talk to a portion of Facebook and only a portion of your followers. Even if one of your followers shares your post with their followers, you're still only reaching a portion of their followers too. With Twitter, you could potentially reach all 255 million active users. Imagine how much it would cost you to place an advertisement in a newspaper with a subscription of 255 million?

I could show you how to create and post one of those tweets quite easily right now but one message won't get you very far. In fact, posting one every day won't get you very far either. You need to be sending tweets hourly. Now I know that seems daunting. Creating just one good tweet can be daunting for many people let alone 24. Let alone 168 to keep you going for the whole week. Let alone being awake to send them out 24 hours a day, 7 days a week. Let alone what your Twitter followers will think of you sending out that many tweets. Seems ridiculous right? Relax. You're going to love this.

It is a little complicated though and it will take you a few days to set up properly, but once you're done, you'll be able to kick back for the next decade with a selection of 100,000 different tweets all going out automatically in random order. All sending a Stampede of customers to your Amazon buy now button. Sound good? Are you up for it? Three days of work?

OK, here we go.

How an Author Should Set Up their Twitter Account

The first thing you need is a Twitter account with a username and password, so if you don't already have one, here's my recommendations.

Use your name, @JoeBlow, or something as close to it as possible. I use @Urban_Hunters which reflects my Urban Hunters book series, but that was due to bad advice early in my career. I've also registered @GaryMTaaffe but I don't use it because my @Urban_Hunters username has become so popular with over 10,000 followers that I'd be mad not to use it. But don't think for a second that it's those 10,000 followers who are getting me so many hits. It's not. You'll see why soon.

As an author, your name is your brand, not your book so think long term. If you are only ever going to write one book, then OK, use your book's name. People won't remember your name until you've got a heap of books out anyway but you do have to *try* to get them to remember your name. It's only then that your name as a brand becomes valuable.

So once you've set up your Twitter account, add a great profile picture, of yourself, not your book, and you're ready for the next step of Stampede.

How to Create Great Eye–Catching Tweets

Your tweets need three elements to make Stampede successful:

- You need to say something entertaining and intriguing. I know, back to the original introvert problem but don't worry, if you're an author, your book already contains everything you need.

- You'll also need your Universal Book Link, or whatever link it is you want to use.

- And you'll need to add a good selection of popular hashtags relevant to your book.

What you're going to do with these three elements is create lots and lots of short sharp advertisements. You're not starting a conversation and being social, you're simply creating an advertisement with a link to your book. The hashtags will spread your advertisements far and wide, and at the same time they'll find focused customers who are interested in your particular type of book.

Hashtags have followers, lots and lots and lots of followers. That's three lots, that's a lot! So if you put a hashtag like #YoungAdult into your tweet, then everyone who follows the #YoungAdult hashtag will also see your tweet.

If you had no followers at all and you posted a tweet, then in all likelihood no one would see it. But when you add #YoungAdult to your tweet, suddenly thousands, possibly millions of people might see it. Add another four or five hashtags and the size of your audience can be staggering. So do you see how you don't need any of your own followers at all to market your book on Twitter?

Here's an example of one of my old tweets that needs some improvements.

Gary Taaffe @urban hunters · 15m
her sniping skills now outstripped her rifle�s capabilities getbook.at/FSe #Sniper #Girls #Grief
View summary

I won't go into how it could be improved now, but I would like you to come back later to see how you'd improve it.

In the meantime, I will mention the strange little question mark in the top right hand corner. That was originally an apostrophe but Twitter seems to handle grammatical marks like these inconsistently. Sometimes quotations marks and apostrophes and dashes work and sometimes they won't. So you have to decide whether or not to use them at all.

As an author, I don't want people thinking that I don't know how to use apostrophes, which is likely to happen if I leave them out. If I leave them in and that funny character appears, I think people are more likely to blame Twitter than me so I leave them in. Plus, if I leave them in, someone might figure out how to fix the problem and all will be well.

That being said, I don't bother with quotation marks at all as I really don't think they're necessary for the quotes in my tweets.

Here's another example of a bad tweet. Actually, a terrible tweet might be a better description of it because I have no clue what this tweet is about and I'm inclined to think that link would lead me to a virus.

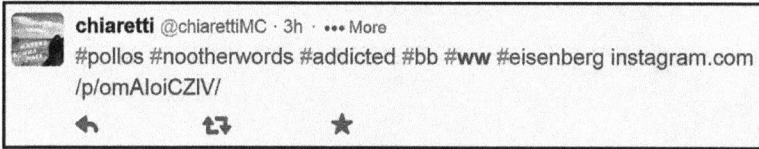

chiaretti @chiarettiMC · 3h · ••• More
#pollos #nootherwords #addicted #bb #ww #eisenberg instagram.com
/p/omAloiCZlV/

It's getting harder and harder to get people to click Twitter links because of tweets like the one above. The good news is that it's easier for people like me who know how to develop well crafted tweets that grab the attention of the casual passerby enough to get them to click my book link.

Let's put some tweets together and I'll explain more about what we're doing as we progress.

Tweets Authors can use Without Being a Social Guru

- Quotes from your book
- Testimonials from readers, fans and reviewers
- News like, New Release
- Book descriptions
- Writing hints and tips and tricks

Quotes from your Book:

As authors, we're really proud of some of our great sentences. Pure gems of Shakespearean genius. If only we could fill the whole book with them but alas, few of us can. We like to think that if we showed those few moments of genius then surely everyone would want to buy our book. Until now we couldn't show those great sentences because taken out of context, they don't make very good book blurbs. And randomly putting great sentences after your blurb on the back of your book would look ridiculous, egotistical even which is more likely to turn a potential customer off. Well the good news is that with Twitter, those great sentences are perfect for marketing. They're interesting and intriguing and that is exactly what you want because that is what gets people to click your Universal Book Link that you've put right beside your genius sentence. So pull out your best sentences, or even part sentences. The shorter the better.

Also, pull out quotes that will pique the interest of certain types or groups of people like horse riders or hunters. In that situation, the quote doesn't have to be a beautifully written sentence, it just has to pique the interest of the people in those groups. Here's a few of mine:

- A torrent of warm blood flowed over her cold fist, soaking her soul in the gentle embrace of a warm bath

- A kiddie sized single shot .22 with open sights

- Amber could only stare while holding back a fearful tear

- We need to talk, Amber, Jim said with a heavy heart

The first one, "A torrent of warm blood …", is a great quote but it's so long that I'll only be able to attach one or two hashtags to it, so I won't get much value out of it. In situations like this, I'll include only very short hashtags like this:

A torrent of warm blood flowed over her cold fist, soaking her soul in the gentle embrace of a warm bath **http://getbook.at/FSc** #YA #Teen

That's 136 characters out of a possible 140 characters that Twitter allows you in each tweet, so it's near enough to perfect. For now that is, we've still got some research ahead of us before we can settle on it though.

I could also shorten the quote up to the comma, creating another tweet and room for more hashtags, which is what I want.

Another thing to consider is Twitter's anti–spamming rules. If all the tweets you send out contain links, that's spamming. So a long quote like this without room for a link would be good simply to entertain the twitter community. As you saw in the example of my tweet that needed improvements, my name and username are all a part of the tweet so if someone was intrigued enough, they could simply click my name and get to my profile where they'll find links to my books.

Another good way of avoiding Twitter's anti–spamming rules and ensuring all your tweets don't have links is to retweet your friends tweets. If someone retweets your tweets, go into their profile from time to time and retweet some of their entertaining tweets. They'll really appreciate it and so will your followers, if you have any.

Testimonials from Readers, Fans and Reviewers:

- I would read ANYTHING this man wrote. NEW YORK BOOK REVIEW, W. D LaRue

- Masterpiece. A must read. Ann Cook, UK

The good thing about testimonials is word–of–mouth is the pinnacle of marketing, and there's no better place for word–of–mouth to take off than on Twitter.

People may not know who W.D LaRue is, or who Ann Cook is either, but they don't have to. Sure, it helps if they do but it's not essential for word–of–mouth to work.

Twitter is full of unknown people recommending things to unknown people. That's one of the things that has made Twitter so popular. Average Joe Blows recommending things to other average Joe Blows. Advice from real down–to–earth people who want to be seen as the person who recommends the good stuff, in the hope of gaining followers.

A great thing about the testimonial by W.D LaRue is I can associate it with any of my books, which is exactly what I'll do. I'll put that quote into a tweet and vary which Universal Book Link I use with it. Basically I'm experimenting to see if one book triggers a sale from that quote better than another book. I'd really like to just send people to the first in my series because it's best if customers start at the beginning, but one cover may pique their interest better than another and the only way I'm going to find out which, is to experiment.

Experimentation is one of the golden rules of marketing so get used to experimenting with your tweets because it can make a massive difference. My Stampede system wouldn't have come into existence if I hadn't been experimenting.

News:

Here are some examples from book eight of my Urban Hunters series:

- New Release FINAL STRAW

- New Release FINAL STRAW Amber's story

- New Release FINAL STRAW A great coming–of–age adventure

- New Release FINAL STRAW How Amber ended up in a rat infested alley in her pyjamas

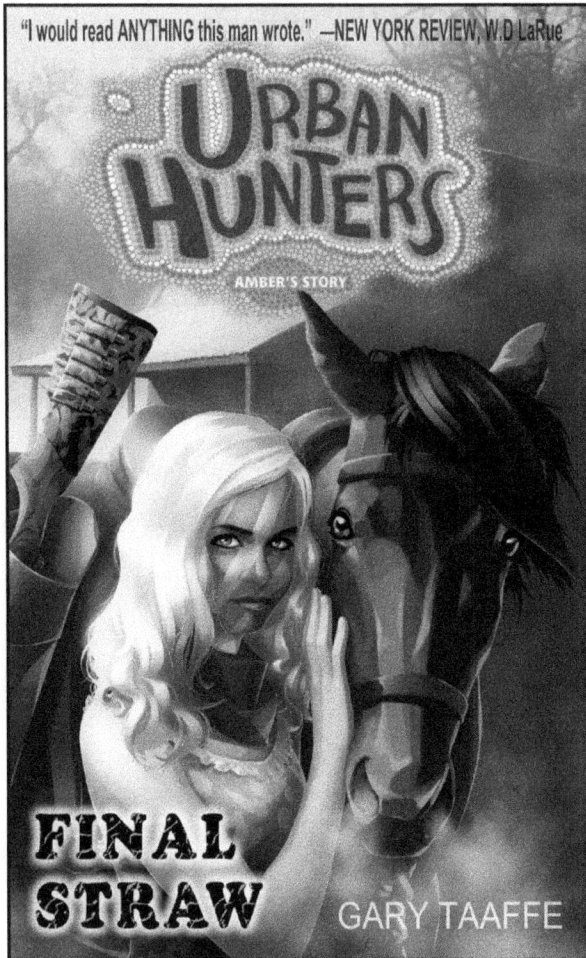

Book Descriptions:

- It was all so perfect, until the dark side of life paid Amber a visit.

- She must decide, kill him now or later? FINAL STRAW

- Remain a victim at the hands of her mother or fight for a life of her own?

These are taken directly from my book's blurb. In coming up with a blurb for your book you'll write lots of little sentences like these but you can't use them all in your blurb no matter how good they are because you've only got so much room, but you can make use of them in your tweets.

Notice in the second example how I've put the title after the intriguing statement? That's because the statement will grab people's attention better than the title will. In the end I didn't even put the title in the tweet because: I decided it was more important to save the space for hashtags, and I felt the statement was better without the title, FINAL STRAW.

Writing Hints and Tips and Tricks:

- Write for the fun of it.

- Start writing and see where it takes you. Discovery is exciting.

- I killed off one of my characters today. Dragged the trauma right out. So fun to write. **http://getbook.at/We**

I've got lots of these little gems. People love hints and tips. This is my opportunity to give back. I don't care if my links aren't clicked or if I don't have links in these tweets at all, I'm just happy to inspire someone. Although I'm not being completely selfless when I do include my link. And I'm being tricky in saying "Write for the fun of it." which is a subliminal message saying my books are fun, which they are.

The third example relates to the third book in my series so I've pointed the link directly to that book.

There are lots of other types of tweets that you can use and experiment with but these will get you off to a fine start.

Hashtag Science

I've used hashtags that I thought would be fine, but upon further research, they turned out to be a waste of time, completely wrong and sometimes, a big no no.

My Urban Hunters series fits fairly and squarely into the Young Adult genre. So I added #YA and #Teens to my tweets. I came back sometime later to experiment and punched #Teens into the Twitter search bar to see how popular #Teens was compared to #YA. Turns out #Teens was much more popular, but it was all about pornography! I'd been marketing my wholesome Young Adult books throughout the sex industry. Needless to say, I removed that hashtag immediately.

Another time I was researching #Shoot and #Snipe because my books have hunting and some sniping in them. It turns out that #Shoot is very popular but it's more about shooting basketball hoops than anything else and #Snipe is all about sniping workers from other companies.

So I soon found out that hashtags needed a little science applied to them. I had to find out not only what were the best hashtags to use but if some combinations of hashtags worked better than others. I'll give you an example.

STAMPEDE

Most of my books are filled with laugh–out–loud humour, they're for Young Adults and there's hunting and cooking of game meat in them. Here's a great tweet for my market:

His tummy told him that ONE RAT JUST WASN'T GOING TO BE ENOUGH **http://getbook.at/We** #YA #lol #Hunting #BBQ #Gamemeat

Not only is there an intriguing story in that quote, but there's a story in the hashtag group as well. And it's only 116 characters so I could fit more hashtags in there if I really wanted to like #ComingOfAge and #Survival. Can you imagine how many people might see that tweet with all those great hashtags?

That's the basics of what we're about to get into, with a couple of extra tricks along the way, so take a big breath because this is where it gets complicated.

What you need to do now is collect a list of hashtags that are relevant to your book. You also need to know how popular they are and what other hashtags are used with those hashtags, or in other words, what hashtags are related to those hashtags.

It used to take me forever to do this through Twitter but as it turns out, I'm not the only one realising the science behind hashtags. Specialist websites have popped up to break down the mystery into exactly the information we need to build a good Stampede strategy.

HASHTAG SCIENCE

Hashtagify.me is my favourite and here's a screenshot in Table Mode using a youngadult search.

Hashtag	Popularity
#youngadult	42.5
#YA	63.0
#paranormal	59.5
#fantasy	64.2
#Kindle	72.6
#IAN1	63.9
#amreading	60.4
#author	62.2
#romance	70.1
#books	69.1
#teen	77.2

There are only two columns that I'm interested in: the hashtag column and the popularity column. I'm also interested in related hashtags which are listed after #YoungAdult. In other words, when people put #YoungAdult into their tweet, the other hashtags on the above list are often seen in the same tweets.

OK so you can see that #YoungAdult has a popularity of 42 (out of 100). And happily, #YA is more popular at 63. That's good news because it only uses 3 characters out of my 140 characters whereas #YoungAdult takes up 11. I list them along with their popularity and see what else there is that I think will be useful.

#Teen is very popular at 77 but for reasons mentioned earlier, I'll be using it sparingly. While I'm on #Teen, I do a quick test on #Teens because that little "s" can sometimes make a big difference. It turns out that it's less popular at 62 and still about sex.

Back to my #YoungAdult search.

#Paranormal and #Fantasy don't apply to me but #IAN1 does because it stands for Independent Author Network. Authors help each other so: I might get some retweets, authors read so I might get some sales and authors buy books for research so again, I might get some sales. I'll have to be careful I don't spam that tag though. I'll talk more about spamming in my Spam Check chapter later but for now, I want to give you a better understanding of hashtags.

#Kindle is an obvious winner considering I'm selling Kindle books and it has a high popularity.

#AmReading is another good word–of–mouth hashtag but it's around the 60 mark so again, I'll have to check that I'm not spamming it.

#Author is similar to #IAN1 and might be helpful occasionally. And #Authors is less popular at 59 but still worth using occasionally for the possibility of reaching a different audience. People who follow #Author may not realise that #Authors exists.

#Books is quite popular at 69 so I'll be sure to add that to my list and of course, I do a search on #Book.

So I've made the most of that list and I'd like to see what a #YA search reveals because that is my main genre after all. Hashtags associated with

#YA are: #Kindle, #Fantasy, #TheFirstPillar, #ASMSG, #EpicFantasy, #Paranormal, #Everyville, #Book, #Romance, #Bestseller.

It hasn't really helped so I move on. An up and coming category within Amazon is #ComingOfAge and I use it often on Amazon so I search that … It's there, written like this: #ComingOfAge, not that the capitals make any difference to the actual hashtag, caps or not they're all the same. Though I do like the way the caps in this case, make the term stand out so I'll use that myself, just as I do with #YA. I'll leave #lol as is because not many people write: LOL.

Interestingly in the same list is #Amazon, at a whopping 79, which I add to my booksellers list and note a strange hashtag: #NewAdult at 48. I haven't seen that one before and it's more popular than #YoungAdult at 42. That changes things. So now #NewAdult is my second favourite after #YA.

Spelling turns out to be a problem with #Humor at 68 and #Humour at 55, which is how us Aussies and the Poms like to spell it. Most of my sales come from Australia so #Humour is important to me. However, with USA being the biggest market by a long shot, I don't want to miss the opportunity of breaking into that market so I'll use both. I won't however, use both in the same tweet.

After all my umming and aahing over #Humor and #Humour, I discovered that both trail a long way behind #lol. A great discovery at only 3 characters. So #lol and #YA are going to be working hard for me. Although I'll have to ensure I don't overuse them and annoy the people following those two hashtags— Spam Check.

Riding the Pig
(or PiggyBacking for the traditionalists amongst you).

If your book is similar to another book, author, movie or subject that's bouncing around Twitter, don't be afraid to jump on that bandwagon. If you think people who read Harry Potter books will like your book too, then throw the odd #HarryPotter or #JKRowling into your tweets. Be creative and resourceful.

So you see where I'm going with all of this. It goes on for quite some time until I have a long list of hashtags all nicely organised. To help me decide which ones to use, I sort them by way of popularity within their subjects. That's when I'm finally ready to move onto the next stage of the process.

If you've been doing some of the things I've suggested as you progressed through this book, this is where I'd suggest you simply read on from here. You'll save yourself a lot of time in the end if you have a better understanding of the process in its entirety.

Unlimited
Tweet Generator

Now that you have your quotes and testimonials etc, your Universal Link and your hashtags, you'll need to group your hashtags and then run them through my Tweet Generator.

Before we get into the science of grouping your hashtags, I want to show you what we're going to do with those hashtag groups, so I think a quick Tweet Generator tutorial will be helpful.

My Tweet Generator mixes and matches hashtagged words creating a long list of varied tweets that you can use with an AutoTweet Program. Study the following image to help you understand how it works.

Unlimited Tweet Generator

Text:

[She must decide, KILL HIM NOW OR LATER? http://getbook.at/FSe] [#MustRead|#NYTimes|#GoodReads] [#Amazon|#BookClub] [#YA|#KidLit|#MGLit|#COA|#Adventure|#Survival] [#Death|#Loss|#Pain] [#Mom|#Family] [#RunAway] [#Daughter|#Girl]

Generate | Delete Tweets | Save Tweets

Output:

She must decide, KILL HIM NOW OR LATER? http://getbook.at/FSe #MustRead #Amazon #YA #Death #Mom #RunAway #Daughter
She must decide, KILL HIM NOW OR LATER? http://getbook.at/FSe #MustRead #Amazon #YA #Death #Mom #RunAway #Girl
She must decide, KILL HIM NOW OR LATER? http://getbook.at/FSe #MustRead #Amazon #YA #Death #Family #RunAway #Daughter
She must decide, KILL HIM NOW OR LATER? http://getbook.at/FSe #MustRead #Amazon #YA #Death #Family #RunAway #Girl
She must decide, KILL HIM NOW OR LATER? http://getbook.at/FSe #MustRead #Amazon #YA #Loss #Mom #RunAway #Daughter
She must decide, KILL HIM NOW OR LATER? http://getbook.at/FSe #MustRead #Amazon #YA #Loss #Mom #RunAway #Girl
She must decide, KILL HIM NOW OR LATER? http://getbook.at/FSe #MustRead #Amazon #YA #Loss #Family #RunAway #Daughter
She must decide, KILL HIM NOW OR LATER? http://getbook.at/FSe #MustRead #Amazon #YA #Loss #Family #RunAway #Girl
She must decide, KILL HIM NOW OR LATER? http://getbook.at/FSe #MustRead #Amazon #YA #Pain #Mom #RunAway #Daughter

As you can see, my quote and link is contained within the first set of brackets, with groups of hashtagged words contained within other sets of brackets. The generator mixes and matches the hashtagged words, or anything separated by the | symbol and the brackets, creating lots and lots of different tweets.

The example, "She must decide, kill him now or later …", with those hashtags creates 433 different tweets. That's too many for most tweets but it is a good eye-catching tweet so I left it as is. You'll be doing the same thing will all of your other quotes and testimonials etc which in the end, will create a very, very long list of tweets. You'll then import those into an AutoTweet program that will send out one tweet per hour in random order 24 hours per day, 7 days per week.

My original Tweet Generator could only use three hashtags which is what I used to discover this amazingly successful Stampede system. But it wasn't long before I decided that I wanted more. So I developed the Unlimited Tweet Generator that you see in the example. It can handle any number of hashtags. If you're happy to use just three hashtags then my original Tweet Generator is available for free for everyone to use at **BunyaPublishing.com**. However if you want to step up a little, then my Unlimited Tweet Generator is also available there, along with a very handy little bonus.

UNLIMITED TWEET GENERATOR

Now at this stage you may be wondering what your followers, Twitter, and anyone else is going to think about you sending out all those advertising tweets, and especially, so many similar tweets. Well if you do it right, no one is going to mind at all because they won't be seeing the same tweet twice. I'll get deeper into that in Spam Check but for now, let me explain who will see what.

Suffer the Consequences! Really? Who Says?

WHAT YOUR FOLLOWERS WILL SEE

When you're viewing your Twitter home page, the latest tweets of the people or companies you are following come up on your screen for you to scroll through and read if you wish. After about a minute, a message comes up telling you how many more tweets have been posted in the last minute for you to view, if you wish. In the time it took me to write that sentence, another 40 tweets came up on mine. There are too many tweets from all the people I follow to keep up with. If someone follows me, I follow them back out of courtesy, but that doesn't mean I read their tweets. It's the same with people who follow me, they don't read all my tweets. My tweets scroll through their tweet feed at a rate of one every hour and they may or may not see it. Actually, it's more than likely they won't. So why would my followers care about me sending out one commercial tweet every hour? They don't. And if they do, they can simply unfollow me or mute my tweets.

Sometimes my followers will drop into my Twitter page to see what I've been posting. If I've done my job correctly, they'll see a variety of interesting and entertaining tweets. More often than not, they'll retweet one or more of my tweets to help me out and to give their followers something interesting to read. And I'll do the same for them. That's word–of–mouth marketing and that is what we all want.

WHAT OTHERS WILL SEE

The only other time anyone on Twitter will see what I've posted is if they're following a hashtag that I've used in my tweet. They'll punch #YA into the Twitter search bar and the #YA tweets will feed onto their screen, with the most popular listed at the top (the ones that have been retweeted or replied to). Or they can adjust the feed to show every single tweet with that hashtag in real time. If I'm really really lucky, they'll see mine, which will pop up at a rate of one per hour.

Knowing this, you may be tempted to increase your tweet rate but Twitter will suspend your account for spamming, so I don't recommend you do that. I'm getting great results with my method as it is so follow my guidelines and consider one per hour a maximum.

What you're better off doing than increasing your tweet rate is fine-tuning your hashtag groups to send focused customers to your door who are more likely to buy. You don't want the average Joe Blow clicking on your link out of curiosity and finding nothing there that interests him. You want people who are going to be interested in your book. #YA has heaps of different genres under it so if you write romance, add #Romance to another hashtag group to tell people that the link will take them to a romantic young adult book. That's the basics, I'll show you how to focus your tweets even further than that in the next chapter.

SUFFER THE CONSEQUENCES! REALLY? WHO SAYS?

So getting back to the chances of people seeing the same tweets twice. My current tweet list is made up of two hundred different quotes and testimonials etc with my Unlimited Tweet Generator generating 111,851 tweets. They're all sent out in random order so I think the chances of the same tweet with different hashtags being sent out one after the other is extremely remote, let alone the chance of anyone noticing it at only one coming through per hour.

The only time I need to be careful is for hashtags that are not used very often. For example if a hashtag is only used say 10 times in a week, and 4 of those are my tweets, someone is going to see me as a spammer and I don't want that. So what I do is search the hashtags I'm using to be sure that isn't happening. If it is, I'll either stop using that hashtag altogether or I'll alter my hashtag groupings so my Unlimited Tweet Generator doesn't produce so many tweets with that hashtag in it. I'll show you how to do that shortly.

It's tricky because you want to spread your tweets far and wide and part of that is using rarely used hashtags relevant to your book. In a way, those rarely used hashtags are gold because the chances of your tweet being seen within that hashtag group are astronomically higher. For example, blacksmithing is important in my books because it gives my characters the ability to make their own weapons to hunt street meat with. So I'll be using #Blacksmith in some of my tweets. Occasionally, someone interested in blacksmithing just might search that hashtag and the chances of them discovering my books that contain the very subject they're interested in is very high. On the other hand, the chances of my tweets being seen in the stream of an extremely busy hashtag like romance, is very low indeed. This is one of the reasons why I say that hashtags can be a bit of a science. And it's good to think of them that way because it puts you into a scientific frame of mind that allows you to slow down and think them through.

So now that you see what's going to happen to your hashtags, it's time to group them to make them as effective as possible.

Hashtag Sentences

I've seen it repeated ad nauseam: "Don't use more than three hashtags in your tweets." They're saying this because so many people are using hashtags badly. The problem is that no one is telling people how to use them well. So that's what I'm going to do here. I've worked out what works and what doesn't and I say, no one is going to mind how many hashtags you use as long as you use them well.

Create Hashtag Sentences that tell a story. A story that ads information to your message to help people understand what it is you're saying or selling.

That way they'll be much more inclined to follow the link in your message. And when they do follow your link, they'll be much more likely to buy because they already know they're interested in your product.

If you choose your hashtags well, they'll filter through the crowds to find very focused customers. Customers who read your type of book. Customers interested in the subject you're writing about.

That's how you multiply the value of hashtags. By combining them with other meaningful hashtags so when someone sees a hashtag that interests them, and the one beside it is another hashtag that interests them, then the two hashtags multiply each other's value. Do that with 5 hashtags in an easy to understand sentence and they multiply each other's value exponentially. If they add to the understanding of your message, then you have gold. You might as well use a link that sends them straight to the deposit section of your bank account.

IN A NUTSHELL

Be selective about your hashtags. Arrange them into hashtag sentences to multiply the value of your hashtags. This multiplies the value of your message, which increases your click through rate and increases the chance of you getting the sale.

Here's a good eye–catching tweet with a poor group of hashtags:

His tummy told him that ONE RAT JUST WASN'T GOING TO BE ENOUGH **http://getbook.at/We** #YA #YoungAdult #NewAdult #Teen #ComingOfAge

Those hashtags draw down heavily on young adults but it doesn't tell them much more about what you're selling. Clearly it's a book because the YA hashtag tells them that and the link tells them that by way of "getbook.at", but it doesn't tell them that it's a humorous story, or that there's hunting in it. The hashtag sentence needs to be a lot more specific to get a good click to sale ratio.

Here's a much better group that's also a great Hashtag Sentence:

His tummy told him that ONE RAT JUST WASN'T GOING TO BE ENOUGH **http://getbook.at/We** #YA #lol #Hunting #BBQ #GameMeat

That tweet will reach young adult readers who are looking for a laugh, who are into hunting, and who like barbecuing game meat. It's very focused on my audience and is an advertisement that is much more likely to get the sale.

HASHTAG SENTENCES

This is the sort of thing you need to do to make the most of each and every tweet.

If after following through with this process, your Amazon Book Page is getting lots and lots of hits but no sales, you're doing something wrong. It might be your tweets, your book's cover, title, subject, blurb or price. It could be lots of things but of one thing I'm certain, if Stampede is sending hundreds of people into your bookstore each and every day and none of them are buying, you're doing something wrong. Stop what you're doing and fix it.

Another reason why you need to think carefully about your hashtag groups is my Unlimited Tweet Generator will generate far more tweets than is useful to you. One quote with seven groups of hashtags could easily generate over 10,000 tweets. Times that by one hundred of your best quotes and testimonials and the next thing you know you've got 1,000,000 tweets. That's too many. You can't manage them effectively and they won't work as well for you as what 100,000 hard–hitting tweets will.

You will never use all of those 100,000 tweets, but it is good to have a large variety to reduce the risk of your randomising AutoPilot program sending out the same message twice in a row.

How to Create Great Hashtag Sentences

When you start collecting hashtags appropriate to your book, you'll find you have far too many to use all at once, so what you need to do is tailor your hashtags and your hashtag groups to each and every quote. Let's break one down into the type of finely tuned detail that will get you loads and loads of sales:

WE NEED TO TALK, AMBER, Jim said with a heavy heart **http://getbook.at/FSe**

That's a father and daughter talking in book 8 of my Urban Hunters series called FINAL STRAW, so let's see what we can grab from my hashtag list.

#Dad is a clear winner with a popularity of 59, compared to #Father at 53. However this quote seems more fatherly to me. Some words evoke the perfect emotional feeling or connection you're going for which is why I think #Father #Daughter will work better than #Dad #Daughter. I compared the two on hashtagify.me and I can't see a difference. Ordinarily the numbers would win the day but I'm pretty set on getting a hashtag sentence of #Father #Daughter. Thankfully, #Daughter rated quite well at 54.

I'll list #Father and #Dad for now and see how many hashtags I end up with in this tweet:

[#Father|#Dad] [#Daughter]

He's also a parent and #Parenting rates well at 62 so I'll definitely add that:

[#Father|#Dad|#Parenting] [#Daughter]

It's also a family thing and that's really popular at 75 so that's in:

[#Father|#Dad|#Parenting|#Family] [#Daughter]

Amber's not only a daughter but she's a girl too so let's see what we get.

Both #Girl and #Girls have a popularity of 71 so I'm torn between them. I think I'll punch each into hashtagify.me to see what their associations are … Turns out porn is associated with both but definitely more so with #Girls. #Girl isn't so bad so I think I'll put it in and see how it goes. Surely young girls on Twitter these days are savvy enough to filter out the porn to find the things they're interested in.

[#Father|#Dad|#Parenting|#Family] [#Daughter|#Girl]

It's the powerful things that Amber has to deal with in this story that make it such a good story so those subjects will have to be added. Alcoholism, death, loss, grief, run away, street kid:

[#Drunk|#AA] both score well and look like good choices for alcoholism.

[#Sad|#Pain|#Death|#Loss|#Grief] all look good for those emotions, in order of popularity.

[#RunAway|#StreetKid] look good for kids who have run away but street kid has a very low popularity at only 13, so if anything has to go, that will be the first.

[#Father|#Dad|#Parenting|#Family] [#Daughter|#Girl] [#Drunk|#AA] [#Sad|#Pain|#Death|#Loss|#Grief] [#RunAway|#StreetKid]

Genre has to be added so this is what I came up with:

[#YA|#YALit|#KidLit|#MGLit|#MG|#ComingOfAge|#Adventure|#Survival]

Collecting all my hashtag groups together so far we get:

[#Father|#Dad|#Parenting|#Family] [#Daughter|#Girl] [#Drunk|#AA] [#Sad|#Pain|#Death|#Loss|#Grief] [#RunAway|#StreetKid] [#YA|#YALit|#KidLit|#MGLit|#MG|#ComingOfAge|#Adventure|#Survival]

TIME TO SADDLE UP THE PIG

An internet newspaper added me to their paper over the weekend simply because I added #HungerGames to some of my tweets. It's perfect for my books because anyone who likes Hunger Games will also like my books.

Here's the internet newspaper with the second image showing three listings for my books after scrolling down the newspaper's front page.

Three separate mentions of my books all on the front cover of that newspaper! I was over the moon about it but then they added another three listings to the following day's newspaper.

And if that wasn't enough, they put me in for a third day running. Plus they also put me in another more visible section. I haven't reprinted the third day's insertion for you here but I'm sure you get the idea. I bet my bottom dollar they'll do it again. Update: They did! That's four days running. Woo hoo.

HEADLINES 📷 PHOTOS ▶ VIDEOS ART & ENTERTAINMENT LE

LEISURE

AP News : Donald Sutherland, Francis Lawrence, Liam Hemsworth, Jennifer Lawrence, Sam Clafin, Josh Hutcherson

AP Shared by
AP Entertainment

m.apnews.com - From left, actor Donald Sutherland, director Francis Lawrence, actors Liam Hemsworth, Jennifer Lawrence, Sam Clafin and Josh Hutcherson pose for photographers during a photo call for Hunger Games: ...

Maps To The Stars France: Julianne Moore & la distribution d'Hunger Games à Cannes [17.05.2014] / Julianne Moore & Hunger Games' cast at Cannes [17.05.2014]

Shared by
MapsToTheStarsFr

mapstothestarsfrance.blogspot.com - Julianne Moore faisait la promotion

drAke SAmpLEz lAuryN HilL, lOVez jeNNIFEr lawrENCE On 'drAFt daY'

Shared by
Teh LA Times

Budgie Smugglers: Billy's Gotta Survive the City eBook: Gary Taaffe: Amazon.fr: Boutique Kindle

Shared by
Gary Taaffe

Bowels of Hell: Billy's Gotta Survive the City eBook: Gary Taaffe: Amazon.fr: Boutique Kindle

Shared by
Gary Taaffe

Four Small Stones eBook: Gary Taaffe: Amazon.fr: Boutique Kindle

Shared by
Gary Taaffe

The lesson here is something I learned many years ago and that is that newspapers and magazines begin each publication with completely blank pages that need to be filled. More often than not, they're grateful if you send them something to fill them up with.

A FRENCH TWIST

N otice how the links to my books in the newspaper are all Amazon France? That tells me that paper.li, the company that hosts all these internet newspapers, for which there are many, must be based in France. I figure the editors have clicked my Universal Links in my tweets and were taken to Amazon France. They've then used my Amazon France book page URL in their newspaper. It would have been better for me if they'd used my actual Universal Links from my tweets, however, beggars can't be choosers. On the plus side it gives me the opportunity to see how many hits I've been getting from these paper.li newspapers. As of today, the little French flags on my BookLinker links tell me I've had over 500 hits! Imagine 500 people standing in your bookshop. That's a pretty packed out bookshop. That's my bookshop! And I'm pretty happy about that.

Interestingly, some of my other books in the Urban Hunters series that weren't mentioned in the newspaper, also got hits from France. Which means they got interested and checked out my other books too.

On top of that, I see they've found their way to my website because those links have been hit by French customers as well.

All in all, I can't ignore the value of putting piggybacking hashtags in my tweets so this is the selection I came up with:

[#HungerGames|#TheFaultInOurStars|#Divergent|#MazeRunner]

And here is everything together:

[WE NEED TO TALK, AMBER, Jim said with a heavy heart **http://getbook.at/FSe**] [#Father|#Dad|#Parenting|#Family] [#Daughter|#Girl] [#Drunk|#AA] [#Sad|#Pain|#Death|#Loss|#Grief] [#RunAway|#StreetKid] [#YA|#YALit|#KidLit|#MGLit|#MG|#ComingOfAge|#Adventure|#Survival] [#HungerGames|#TheFaultInOurStars|#Divergent|#MazeRunner]

Before I go any further, I know from past experience that all those hashtags and groups are going to create far too many tweets. But I'll run it through my Tweet Generator anyway just for the fun of it …

Sure enough, it created 5,121 tweets and my poor computer started smoking ;) Some of those tweets were too long too, so I'll need to remove each and every one of them. Here's a screenshot of another tweet in my text editor showing me how I see how many characters each tweet has. I drew the line in to demonstrate the tweets that will need to be deleted.

My AutoPilot program, or my AutoTweet program, will send out my tweets regardless of how long they are, but Twitter won't accept them if they're more than 140 characters long, so that hour's tweet would be wasted. That's why I have to delete the long tweets. In this case there's 669 of them, leaving me with 4,452 tweets. Still too many so clearly I have to reduce the number of hashtags and/or combine some of the groups.

[WE NEED TO TALK, AMBER, Jim said with a heavy heart **http://getbook.at/FSe**] [#Father|#Dad|#Parenting|#Family] [#Daughter|#Girl] [#Drunk|#AA] [#Sad|#Pain|#Death|#Loss|#Grief] [#RunAway|#StreetKid] [#YA|#YALit|#KidLit|#MGLit|#MG|#ComingOfAge|#Adventure|#Survival|#HungerGames|#TheFaultInOurStars|#Divergent|#MazeRunner]

#Dad is out as is #Death, #Loss and #Grief, and because #Sad and #Pain are more popular and suit my needs for this particular tweet, they get to stay. #StreetKid is out too and in hindsight, I know this tweet will end up being well short of the 140 character mark so I'll save #YA and #MG for tweets that are short on space. #RunAway is really important to this hashtag sentence so I'll put it in brackets on it's own so it ends up in every single tweet. I've also combined my genre and piggybacking hashtags as I figure that with them separated, there will still be too many tweets generated. So I've ended up with the following, that I ran through my Unlimited Tweet Generator:

[WE NEED TO TALK, AMBER, Jim said with a heavy heart
http://getbook.at/FSe] [#Father|#Parenting|#Family] [#Daughter|#Girl]
[#Drunk|#AA] [#Sad|#Pain] [#RunAway]
[#YALit|#KidLit|#MGLit|#ComingOfAge|#Adventure|#Survival|#Hunge
rGames|#TheFaultInOurStars|#Divergent|#MazeRunner]

241 tweets generated— perfect, and here's an example:

WE NEED TO TALK, AMBER, Jim said with a heavy heart
http://getbook.at/FSe #Parenting #Daughter #Drunk #Sad #RunAway
#Survival

Close but that hashtag sentence says that it's the daughter who's
drinking and that's not the case so let's shuffle things around a bit and
do another test:

[WE NEED TO TALK, AMBER, Jim said with a heavy heart
http://getbook.at/FSe] [#Drunk|#AA] [#Father|#Parenting|#Family]
[#Daughter|#Girl] [#Pain|#Sad] [#Runaway]
[#YALit|#KidLit|#MGLit|#ComingOfAge|#Adventure|#Survival|#Hunge
rGames|#TheFaultInOurStars|#Divergent|#MazeRunner]

WE NEED TO TALK, AMBER, Jim said with a heavy heart
http://getbook.at/FSe #Drunk #Parenting #Daughter #Sad #Runaway
#Survival

Woo hoo! How good is that! I'm really excited by that tweet. The
quote tells an intriguing and entertaining story and so do the hashtags.
Not only that but the hashtags expand on the quote by telling more of
the story.

Now we can guess that it was drinking that Jim wanted to talk to
Amber about and that it didn't work because Amber ran away. And now
she has to survive on the street.

But wait, there's more to those 140 characters! Six of those words are
doing double duty because they're coded with the hashtag symbol that
automatically duplicates the tweet six times over, spreading it far and

wide to thousands and thousands more people. That's what I call exponential marketing and it doesn't get any better than that!

So your one tweet containing six hashtags has suddenly turned into seven tweets. Your original, plus one for each hashtag. One gets posted to your timeline and another into each of the hashtag categories. So if each of your tweets contain six hashtags, your original 24 tweets per day has suddenly turned into 168 tweets per day.

How are you feeling about only sending out 24 tweets per day now? You should be feeling a lot better about it. I know I am.

And have you noticed how I've been capitalising some of the text to make it even more hard–hitting. Here it is tweeted.

And here it is favourited by Reddit less than two minutes later!

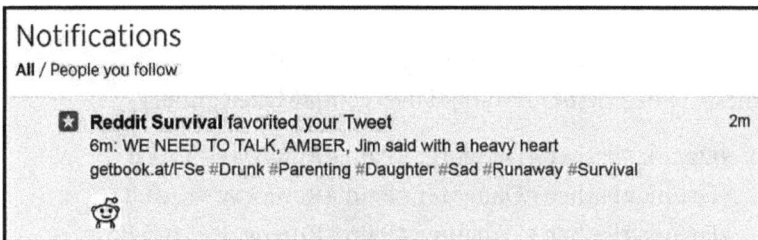

Thank you, @RedditSurvival, your timing was impeccable. Go follow them, folks, they must be some really nice people :)

To be pedantic, that group is going to create some tweets like this: #Drunk #Father #Daughter … So you could think they're both drinking. You could think lots of things with the tweets that are going to be generated. The thing is, it's a father and daughter talking and alcohol is clearly the problem because I've positioned drinking prominently. So not every tweet is going to be perfect, but your potential reader won't mind as long as it's close. After they've become intrigued enough to follow your link, they can read your blurb and decide from there. However, there's no reason why you couldn't go through the list and delete individual tweets that you don't like.

So to be absolutely certain that you understand what has happened here, I'm going to list every single one of those 241 tweets, without the full message and link:

[WE NEED TO TALK, AMBER, Jim said with a heavy heart **http://getbook.at/FSe**] [#Drunk|#AA] [#Father|#Parenting|#Family] [#Daughter|#Girl] [#Pain|#Sad] [#Runaway] [#YALit|#KidLit|#MGLit|#ComingOfAge|#Adventure|#Survival|#HungerGames|#TheFaultInOurStars|#Divergent|#MazeRunner]

WE…#Drunk #Father #Daughter #Pain #Runaway #YALit
WE…#Drunk #Father #Daughter #Pain #Runaway #KidLit
WE…#Drunk #Father #Daughter #Pain #Runaway #MGLit
WE…#Drunk #Father #Daughter #Pain #Runaway #ComingOfAge
WE…#Drunk #Father #Daughter #Pain #Runaway #Adventure
WE…#Drunk #Father #Daughter #Pain #Runaway #Survival
WE…#Drunk #Father #Daughter #Pain #Runaway #HungerGames
WE…#Drunk #Father #Daughter #Pain #Runaway #TheFaultInOurStars

How to Create Great Hashtag Sentences

WE...#Drunk #Father #Daughter #Pain #Runaway #Divergent

WE...#Drunk #Father #Daughter #Pain #Runaway #MazeRunner

WE...#Drunk #Father #Daughter #Sad #Runaway #YALit

WE...#Drunk #Father #Daughter #Sad #Runaway #KidLit

WE...#Drunk #Father #Daughter #Sad #Runaway #MGLit

WE...#Drunk #Father #Daughter #Sad #Runaway #ComingOfAge

WE...#Drunk #Father #Daughter #Sad #Runaway #Adventure

WE...#Drunk #Father #Daughter #Sad #Runaway #Survival

WE...#Drunk #Father #Daughter #Sad #Runaway #HungerGames

WE...#Drunk #Father #Daughter #Sad #Runaway #TheFaultInOurStars

WE...#Drunk #Father #Daughter #Sad #Runaway #Divergent

WE...#Drunk #Father #Daughter #Sad #Runaway #MazeRunner

WE...#Drunk #Father #Girl #Pain #Runaway #YALit

WE...#Drunk #Father #Girl #Pain #Runaway #KidLit

WE...#Drunk #Father #Girl #Pain #Runaway #MGLit

WE...#Drunk #Father #Girl #Pain #Runaway #ComingOfAge

WE...#Drunk #Father #Girl #Pain #Runaway #Adventure

WE...#Drunk #Father #Girl #Pain #Runaway #Survival

WE...#Drunk #Father #Girl #Pain #Runaway #HungerGames

WE...#Drunk #Father #Girl #Pain #Runaway #TheFaultInOurStars

WE...#Drunk #Father #Girl #Pain #Runaway #Divergent

WE...#Drunk #Father #Girl #Pain #Runaway #MazeRunner

WE...#Drunk #Father #Girl #Sad #Runaway #YALit

WE...#Drunk #Father #Girl #Sad #Runaway #KidLit

WE...#Drunk #Father #Girl #Sad #Runaway #MGLit

WE...#Drunk #Father #Girl #Sad #Runaway #ComingOfAge

WE...#Drunk #Father #Girl #Sad #Runaway #Adventure

WE...#Drunk #Father #Girl #Sad #Runaway #Survival

WE...#Drunk #Father #Girl #Sad #Runaway #HungerGames

WE...#Drunk #Father #Girl #Sad #Runaway #TheFaultInOurStars

WE...#Drunk #Father #Girl #Sad #Runaway #Divergent

WE...#Drunk #Father #Girl #Sad #Runaway #MazeRunner

WE...#Drunk #Parenting #Daughter #Pain #Runaway #YALit

WE...#Drunk #Parenting #Daughter #Pain #Runaway #KidLit

WE...#Drunk #Parenting #Daughter #Pain #Runaway #MGLit

WE...#Drunk #Parenting #Daughter #Pain #Runaway #ComingOfAge

WE...#Drunk #Parenting #Daughter #Pain #Runaway #Adventure

WE...#Drunk #Parenting #Daughter #Pain #Runaway #Survival

WE...#Drunk #Parenting #Daughter #Pain #Runaway #HungerGames

WE...#Drunk #Parenting #Daughter #Pain #Runaway
#TheFaultInOurStars

WE...#Drunk #Parenting #Daughter #Pain #Runaway #Divergent

WE...#Drunk #Parenting #Daughter #Pain #Runaway #MazeRunner

WE...#Drunk #Parenting #Daughter #Sad #Runaway #YALit

WE...#Drunk #Parenting #Daughter #Sad #Runaway #KidLit

WE...#Drunk #Parenting #Daughter #Sad #Runaway #MGLit

WE...#Drunk #Parenting #Daughter #Sad #Runaway #ComingOfAge

WE...#Drunk #Parenting #Daughter #Sad #Runaway #Adventure

WE...#Drunk #Parenting #Daughter #Sad #Runaway #Survival

WE...#Drunk #Parenting #Daughter #Sad #Runaway #HungerGames

WE...#Drunk #Parenting #Daughter #Sad #Runaway
#TheFaultInOurStars

WE...#Drunk #Parenting #Daughter #Sad #Runaway #Divergent

WE...#Drunk #Parenting #Daughter #Sad #Runaway #MazeRunner

WE...#Drunk #Parenting #Girl #Pain #Runaway #YALit

WE...#Drunk #Parenting #Girl #Pain #Runaway #KidLit

WE...#Drunk #Parenting #Girl #Pain #Runaway #MGLit

WE...#Drunk #Parenting #Girl #Pain #Runaway #ComingOfAge

WE...#Drunk #Parenting #Girl #Pain #Runaway #Adventure

WE...#Drunk #Parenting #Girl #Pain #Runaway #Survival

WE...#Drunk #Parenting #Girl #Pain #Runaway #HungerGames

WE...#Drunk #Parenting #Girl #Pain #Runaway #TheFaultInOurStars

WE...#Drunk #Parenting #Girl #Pain #Runaway #Divergent

WE...#Drunk #Parenting #Girl #Pain #Runaway #MazeRunner

WE...#Drunk #Parenting #Girl #Sad #Runaway #YALit

WE...#Drunk #Parenting #Girl #Sad #Runaway #KidLit

HOW TO CREATE GREAT HASHTAG SENTENCES

WE…#Drunk #Parenting #Girl #Sad #Runaway #MGLit
WE…#Drunk #Parenting #Girl #Sad #Runaway #ComingOfAge
WE…#Drunk #Parenting #Girl #Sad #Runaway #Adventure
WE…#Drunk #Parenting #Girl #Sad #Runaway #Survival
WE…#Drunk #Parenting #Girl #Sad #Runaway #HungerGames
WE…#Drunk #Parenting #Girl #Sad #Runaway #TheFaultInOurStars
WE…#Drunk #Parenting #Girl #Sad #Runaway #Divergent
WE…#Drunk #Parenting #Girl #Sad #Runaway #MazeRunner
WE…#Drunk #Family #Daughter #Pain #Runaway #YALit
WE…#Drunk #Family #Daughter #Pain #Runaway #KidLit
WE…#Drunk #Family #Daughter #Pain #Runaway #MGLit
WE…#Drunk #Family #Daughter #Pain #Runaway #ComingOfAge
WE…#Drunk #Family #Daughter #Pain #Runaway #Adventure
WE…#Drunk #Family #Daughter #Pain #Runaway #Survival
WE…#Drunk #Family #Daughter #Pain #Runaway #HungerGames
WE…#Drunk #Family #Daughter #Pain #Runaway
#TheFaultInOurStars
WE…#Drunk #Family #Daughter #Pain #Runaway #Divergent
WE…#Drunk #Family #Daughter #Pain #Runaway #MazeRunner
WE…#Drunk #Family #Daughter #Sad #Runaway #YALit
WE…#Drunk #Family #Daughter #Sad #Runaway #KidLit
WE…#Drunk #Family #Daughter #Sad #Runaway #MGLit
WE…#Drunk #Family #Daughter #Sad #Runaway #ComingOfAge
WE…#Drunk #Family #Daughter #Sad #Runaway #Adventure
WE…#Drunk #Family #Daughter #Sad #Runaway #Survival
WE…#Drunk #Family #Daughter #Sad #Runaway #HungerGames
WE…#Drunk #Family #Daughter #Sad #Runaway #TheFaultInOurStars
WE…#Drunk #Family #Daughter #Sad #Runaway #Divergent
WE…#Drunk #Family #Daughter #Sad #Runaway #MazeRunner
WE…#Drunk #Family #Girl #Pain #Runaway #YALit
WE…#Drunk #Family #Girl #Pain #Runaway #KidLit
WE…#Drunk #Family #Girl #Pain #Runaway #MGLit
WE…#Drunk #Family #Girl #Pain #Runaway #ComingOfAge

WE...#Drunk #Family #Girl #Pain #Runaway #Adventure
WE...#Drunk #Family #Girl #Pain #Runaway #Survival
WE...#Drunk #Family #Girl #Pain #Runaway #HungerGames
WE...#Drunk #Family #Girl #Pain #Runaway #TheFaultInOurStars
WE...#Drunk #Family #Girl #Pain #Runaway #Divergent
WE...#Drunk #Family #Girl #Pain #Runaway #MazeRunner
WE...#Drunk #Family #Girl #Sad #Runaway #YALit
WE...#Drunk #Family #Girl #Sad #Runaway #KidLit
WE...#Drunk #Family #Girl #Sad #Runaway #MGLit
WE...#Drunk #Family #Girl #Sad #Runaway #ComingOfAge
WE...#Drunk #Family #Girl #Sad #Runaway #Adventure
WE...#Drunk #Family #Girl #Sad #Runaway #Survival
WE...#Drunk #Family #Girl #Sad #Runaway #HungerGames
WE...#Drunk #Family #Girl #Sad #Runaway #TheFaultInOurStars
WE...#Drunk #Family #Girl #Sad #Runaway #Divergent
WE...#Drunk #Family #Girl #Sad #Runaway #MazeRunner
WE...#AA #Father #Daughter #Pain #Runaway #YALit
WE...#AA #Father #Daughter #Pain #Runaway #KidLit
WE...#AA #Father #Daughter #Pain #Runaway #MGLit
WE...#AA #Father #Daughter #Pain #Runaway #ComingOfAge
WE...#AA #Father #Daughter #Pain #Runaway #Adventure
WE...#AA #Father #Daughter #Pain #Runaway #Survival
WE...#AA #Father #Daughter #Pain #Runaway #HungerGames
WE...#AA #Father #Daughter #Pain #Runaway #TheFaultInOurStars
WE...#AA #Father #Daughter #Pain #Runaway #Divergent
WE...#AA #Father #Daughter #Pain #Runaway #MazeRunner
WE...#AA #Father #Daughter #Sad #Runaway #YALit
WE...#AA #Father #Daughter #Sad #Runaway #KidLit
WE...#AA #Father #Daughter #Sad #Runaway #MGLit
WE...#AA #Father #Daughter #Sad #Runaway #ComingOfAge
WE...#AA #Father #Daughter #Sad #Runaway #Adventure
WE...#AA #Father #Daughter #Sad #Runaway #Survival
WE...#AA #Father #Daughter #Sad #Runaway #HungerGames

HOW TO CREATE GREAT HASHTAG SENTENCES

WE...#AA #Father #Daughter #Sad #Runaway #TheFaultInOurStars
WE...#AA #Father #Daughter #Sad #Runaway #Divergent
WE...#AA #Father #Daughter #Sad #Runaway #MazeRunner
WE...#AA #Father #Girl #Pain #Runaway #YALit
WE...#AA #Father #Girl #Pain #Runaway #KidLit
WE...#AA #Father #Girl #Pain #Runaway #MGLit
WE...#AA #Father #Girl #Pain #Runaway #ComingOfAge
WE...#AA #Father #Girl #Pain #Runaway #Adventure
WE...#AA #Father #Girl #Pain #Runaway #Survival
WE...#AA #Father #Girl #Pain #Runaway #HungerGames
WE...#AA #Father #Girl #Pain #Runaway #TheFaultInOurStars
WE...#AA #Father #Girl #Pain #Runaway #Divergent
WE...#AA #Father #Girl #Pain #Runaway #MazeRunner
WE...#AA #Father #Girl #Sad #Runaway #YALit
WE...#AA #Father #Girl #Sad #Runaway #KidLit
WE...#AA #Father #Girl #Sad #Runaway #MGLit
WE...#AA #Father #Girl #Sad #Runaway #ComingOfAge
WE...#AA #Father #Girl #Sad #Runaway #Adventure
WE...#AA #Father #Girl #Sad #Runaway #Survival
WE...#AA #Father #Girl #Sad #Runaway #HungerGames
WE...#AA #Father #Girl #Sad #Runaway #TheFaultInOurStars
WE...#AA #Father #Girl #Sad #Runaway #Divergent
WE...#AA #Father #Girl #Sad #Runaway #MazeRunner
WE...#AA #Parenting #Daughter #Pain #Runaway #YALit
WE...#AA #Parenting #Daughter #Pain #Runaway #KidLit
WE...#AA #Parenting #Daughter #Pain #Runaway #MGLit
WE...#AA #Parenting #Daughter #Pain #Runaway #ComingOfAge
WE...#AA #Parenting #Daughter #Pain #Runaway #Adventure
WE...#AA #Parenting #Daughter #Pain #Runaway #Survival
WE...#AA #Parenting #Daughter #Pain #Runaway #HungerGames
WE...#AA #Parenting #Daughter #Pain #Runaway
#TheFaultInOurStars
WE...#AA #Parenting #Daughter #Pain #Runaway #Divergent

WE...#AA #Parenting #Daughter #Pain #Runaway #MazeRunner
WE...#AA #Parenting #Daughter #Sad #Runaway #YALit
WE...#AA #Parenting #Daughter #Sad #Runaway #KidLit
WE...#AA #Parenting #Daughter #Sad #Runaway #MGLit
WE...#AA #Parenting #Daughter #Sad #Runaway #ComingOfAge
WE...#AA #Parenting #Daughter #Sad #Runaway #Adventure
WE...#AA #Parenting #Daughter #Sad #Runaway #Survival
WE...#AA #Parenting #Daughter #Sad #Runaway #HungerGames
WE...#AA #Parenting #Daughter #Sad #Runaway #TheFaultInOurStars
WE...#AA #Parenting #Daughter #Sad #Runaway #Divergent
WE...#AA #Parenting #Daughter #Sad #Runaway #MazeRunner
WE...#AA #Parenting #Girl #Pain #Runaway #YALit
WE...#AA #Parenting #Girl #Pain #Runaway #KidLit
WE...#AA #Parenting #Girl #Pain #Runaway #MGLit
WE...#AA #Parenting #Girl #Pain #Runaway #ComingOfAge
WE...#AA #Parenting #Girl #Pain #Runaway #Adventure
WE...#AA #Parenting #Girl #Pain #Runaway #Survival
WE...#AA #Parenting #Girl #Pain #Runaway #HungerGames
WE...#AA #Parenting #Girl #Pain #Runaway #TheFaultInOurStars
WE...#AA #Parenting #Girl #Pain #Runaway #Divergent
WE...#AA #Parenting #Girl #Pain #Runaway #MazeRunner
WE...#AA #Parenting #Girl #Sad #Runaway #YALit
WE...#AA #Parenting #Girl #Sad #Runaway #KidLit
WE...#AA #Parenting #Girl #Sad #Runaway #MGLit
WE...#AA #Parenting #Girl #Sad #Runaway #ComingOfAge
WE...#AA #Parenting #Girl #Sad #Runaway #Adventure
WE...#AA #Parenting #Girl #Sad #Runaway #Survival
WE...#AA #Parenting #Girl #Sad #Runaway #HungerGames
WE...#AA #Parenting #Girl #Sad #Runaway #TheFaultInOurStars
WE...#AA #Parenting #Girl #Sad #Runaway #Divergent
WE...#AA #Parenting #Girl #Sad #Runaway #MazeRunner
WE...#AA #Family #Daughter #Pain #Runaway #YALit
WE...#AA #Family #Daughter #Pain #Runaway #KidLit

HOW TO CREATE GREAT HASHTAG SENTENCES

WE...#AA #Family #Daughter #Pain #Runaway #MGLit
WE...#AA #Family #Daughter #Pain #Runaway #ComingOfAge
WE...#AA #Family #Daughter #Pain #Runaway #Adventure
WE...#AA #Family #Daughter #Pain #Runaway #Survival
WE...#AA #Family #Daughter #Pain #Runaway #HungerGames
WE...#AA #Family #Daughter #Pain #Runaway #TheFaultInOurStars
WE...#AA #Family #Daughter #Pain #Runaway #Divergent
WE...#AA #Family #Daughter #Pain #Runaway #MazeRunner
WE...#AA #Family #Daughter #Sad #Runaway #YALit
WE...#AA #Family #Daughter #Sad #Runaway #KidLit
WE...#AA #Family #Daughter #Sad #Runaway #MGLit
WE...#AA #Family #Daughter #Sad #Runaway #ComingOfAge
WE...#AA #Family #Daughter #Sad #Runaway #Adventure
WE...#AA #Family #Daughter #Sad #Runaway #Survival
WE...#AA #Family #Daughter #Sad #Runaway #HungerGames
WE...#AA #Family #Daughter #Sad #Runaway #TheFaultInOurStars
WE...#AA #Family #Daughter #Sad #Runaway #Divergent
WE...#AA #Family #Daughter #Sad #Runaway #MazeRunner
WE...#AA #Family #Girl #Pain #Runaway #YALit
WE...#AA #Family #Girl #Pain #Runaway #KidLit
WE...#AA #Family #Girl #Pain #Runaway #MGLit
WE...#AA #Family #Girl #Pain #Runaway #ComingOfAge
WE...#AA #Family #Girl #Pain #Runaway #Adventure
WE...#AA #Family #Girl #Pain #Runaway #Survival
WE...#AA #Family #Girl #Pain #Runaway #HungerGames
WE...#AA #Family #Girl #Pain #Runaway #TheFaultInOurStars
WE...#AA #Family #Girl #Pain #Runaway #Divergent
WE...#AA #Family #Girl #Pain #Runaway #MazeRunner
WE...#AA #Family #Girl #Sad #Runaway #YALit
WE...#AA #Family #Girl #Sad #Runaway #KidLit
WE...#AA #Family #Girl #Sad #Runaway #MGLit
WE...#AA #Family #Girl #Sad #Runaway #ComingOfAge
WE...#AA #Family #Girl #Sad #Runaway #Adventure

WE…#AA #Family #Girl #Sad #Runaway #Survival
WE…#AA #Family #Girl #Sad #Runaway #HungerGames
WE…#AA #Family #Girl #Sad #Runaway #TheFaultInOurStars
WE…#AA #Family #Girl #Sad #Runaway #Divergent
WE…#AA #Family #Girl #Sad #Runaway #MazeRunner

That's one quote done. Now to my other 300. Groan. The good news is that the first one is the hardest. I've now got groups of hashtags to copy and paste and I've gotten the hang of doing this.

Past experience tells me that I'll be in for a good two or three days of work. That may seem like a lot but if you told an advertising company that it took you two days to produce 100,000 fantastic ads, they'd think you were mad. Can you imagine how much they'd charge you to produce those ads? And can you imagine how much it would cost you to run those ads? This will only cost you time and it won't be time wasted on social media.

AutoPilot

Now that you have your very long list of tweets, or I do anyway, you need a program to send them out automatically for you. You could do it yourself but you have to sleep sometime, and when you're sleeping, people on the other side of the world are looking for books to buy.

I love **TweetAdder.com**, for which I have a membership. There are other programs out there like HootSuite that do similar things and some that are even free. I see Twitter now also has a tweet scheduler but it's nowhere near good enough for what you'll need to be doing.

TweetAdder does lots of things but all I'm going to be focusing on here is the tweet automation side of it.

Following is an image of the page that does everything you need.

As you'll see, it shows my list of 65,207 tweets. They were generated from my original 324 tweets which averages out to 201 tweets generated from each original tweet. I have eight books on Amazon so that averages out to 40 original tweets per book.

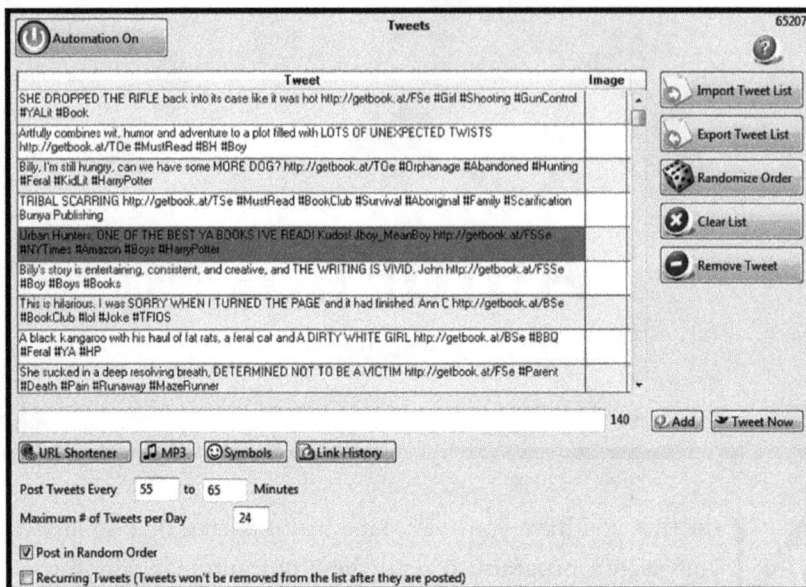

After compiling my 65,207 tweets into a .txt file, I hit the Import Tweet List button in TweetAdder and locate my .txt file on my computer. After it has uploaded into TweetAdder, I hit the Randomize Order button and rerandomize about 10 times to make sure they're well and truly mixed up. Then I tell it to send out a tweet every 55 to 65 minutes with a maximum of 24 tweets per day. I also tell it to send them out in random order and then I hit the Automation On button.

And that's it for the next 24 hours, until I do a Spam Check which I'll cover in the next chapter. I leave the program and my computer running 24 hours a day, 7 days a week.

See how simple this system is? Sure it's been a bit of a stuff around getting it up and running but once it's done, you could forget about it for a whole decade if you wanted to. Personally, I'll be tweaking mine every now and again to find new favourite hashtags and to mix things up. But mostly, I'll be kicking back with time on my hands to write my next book.

Spam Check

So I've had my tweets on AutoPilot for 24 hours and it's time to do a spam check. I go into Twitter and do a search on all the hashtags that I've used, each and every single one of them. I'm looking to make sure that my tweets aren't listed one after the other. If they are, then that's spamming and I most definitely don't want to be doing that. To my horror I see exactly that has happened to #BookReviewers.

I thought #BookReviewers would be a good place for book reviewers to find new books to review. Good in theory, terrible in practice because although #BookReviewers has a popularity of 41, which is OK as long as I don't use it too often, it turns out that it's hardly ever used by anyone else. Now I don't understand how it can have a high popularity when it is hardly ever used but clearly, the popularity number isn't enough to go off. After searching the net for a website that would give me that information, it turned out that hashtagify.me had it perfectly presented in another window. I was using the "Related Hashtags" tab at the top of the hashtagify.me window to check popularity. The "Usage Patterns" tab is where you find usage and #BookReviewers was barely a 1. So in other words, it's barely used once per day. Whoops.

After thinking about it, book reviewers don't need to go looking for books to review anyway because their inbox gets flooded with review requests from authors every single day. So it's no wonder that hashtag is hardly ever used.

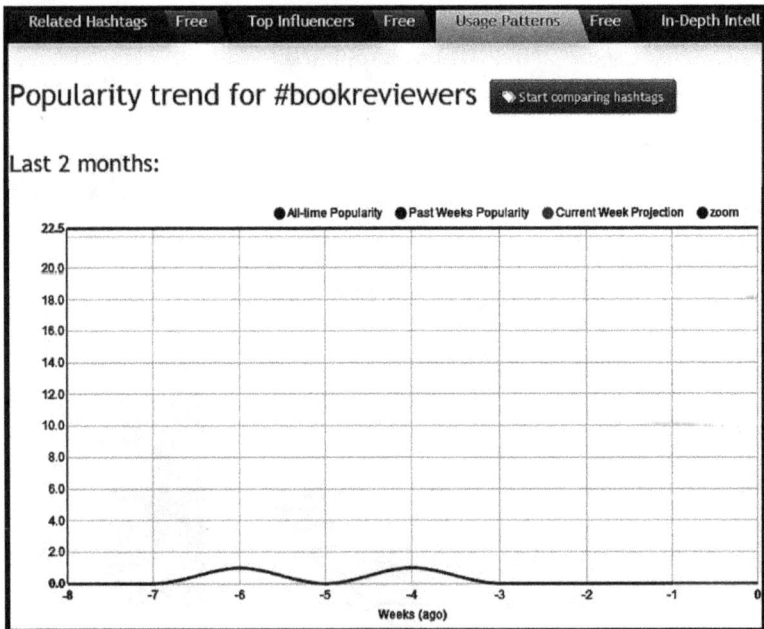

SPAM CHECK

What I had to do then was go through my list of hashtags and give each one a usage number, along with its popularity number. The results were startling. I had to go back and rewrite at least half of my tweets and run them back through my Unlimited Tweet Generator to be sure they weren't too long.

That's why I wanted to you read through the rest of this book before going any further with putting your tweets together. I thought it would be a good lesson for your to see the mistake I made and be reminded that this is a kind of science. You have to think things through, plan ahead.

I made some interesting discoveries along the way. One of them was #COA, which is short for #ComingOfAge. It has a higher popularity than #ComingOfAge and it's only 4 characters. Woo hoo. But it's usage was a bit lower than #ComingOfAge so I ended up finding and replacing half of my #ComingOfAge with #COA.

Another horror story was #LadLit. I realised that I had #YA in nearly every single tweet so I replaced many of them with #LadLit, #YALit and others. I really liked #LadLit because boys love my books and I wanted to reach them. Well, it was this spam checking process that revealed that #LadLit has an appalling usage of only 1. Back to the drawing board.

To count how often you're using the same hashtags, do a find and replace in your main .txt file. Find #YA and replace with #YA. If you've got 60,000 tweets and you've used #YA 60,000 times, then that's too many. Change some of them to #YALit or something like that. Be creative. Experiment.

So after all that, I'm happy to say that my tweets have been tweaked and they're all doing very nicely indeed. In fact I've had a dramatic increase in hits and of course, sales. Clearly the people clicking my Universal Links are now very much more focused and much more likely to buy my books. As difficult and long winded as this whole process has been, it has been very worthwhile indeed.

Dummy Check

Check your tweets for mistakes. Sometimes you might have forgotten the hashtag symbol. I had #YA in two groups so it came up in some of my tweets like this: #YA #YA. And I found that I'd missed the underscore in some @Urban_Hunters. You might not have even done your link correctly. So every now and again, go into Twitter and have a good look at the tweets that have gone out to be sure you haven't made any silly mistakes.

Hashtag Popularity and Usage

Here's a general selection of hashtags relevant to some writers. The first number is popularity, the second is usage and don't forget that these values will change over time depending upon what is trending at the time:

#Teen 75 80
#YA 63 50
#Teens 61 55
#MG 54 35
#KidLit 52 35
#YALit 52 35
#NewAdult 48 30
#COA 44 15
#MGLit 42 25
#YoungAdult 42 21
#ComingOfAge 38 20
#LadLit 28 1

#Writing 66 55
#AmWriting 65 55
#IAN1 63 55
#Author 62 45
#Mustread 60 50
#Writers 59 45
#Authors 59 45
#Writer 59 40
#Writetip 53 35
#NaNoWriMo 52 10
#PubTip 43 20

#AmReading 60 45
#Fiction 58 45

#GoodReads 54 40
#Readers54 35
#GoodRead 48 30

#Amazon 79 79
#Kindle 72 65
#Nook 59 45

#Book 72 60
#Books 69 60
#eBook 67 60

#Win 83 80
#Free 80 75
#GiveAway 79 75
#Competition 74 70
#Contest 67 60

#Adventure 60 50
#Action 58 45
#Survival 55 45

Free and Competitions

PermaFree, or giving away your eBook for free permanently is not a good idea for too many reasons to list here, however, giving away the first in your series is a good idea and this is how I do it:

[HILARIOUS, URBAN HUNTERS survival series, book 1 FREE here
http://bit.ly/11ZMOtt]
[#Free|#Giveaway|#Freebies|#FreeBooks|#FreeKindleBooks]
[#eBook|#Kindle|#Amazon|#Kindle]
[#MustRead|#NYTimes|#BookClub]
[#YA|#YALit|#KidLit|#MG|#MGLit]
[#HungerGames|#CatchingFire|#TFIOS|#TheFaultInOurStars|#HarryPotter|#HP|#MazeRunner|#Divergent|#TheGiver]

And here is a sample from the tweets generated:

HILARIOUS, URBAN HUNTERS survival series, book 1 FREE here
http://bit.ly/11ZMOtt #Free #eBook #MustRead #YA #HungerGames

My goal here is to give away as many of these books as I possibly can, to give readers a taste of my series and my writing.

That group is going to create around 3,000 tweets which is obviously an awful lot. But that only represents 5% of my 60,000 tweets. So if my AutoTweet program is sending 24 random tweets per day, then I can expect one of these free tweets to be going out everyday. Which isn't many really but pushing it any further on Twitter would be too much.

That's where the Amazon Select program comes in handy if you're eligible, which I'm not. So I put a link in that tweet sending people to my website where they can download the first in my series for free in three different formats: .mobi, .epub and .pdf. In exchange I ask for their email address which subscribes them to my newsletter, for which they can unsubscribe at anytime if they wish. Easy peasy.

How to Deal with all your Lovers

H ave you seen the Friday Follow tweets (#FF), or the Worth Watching tweets (#WW)? Here's a #WW tweet.

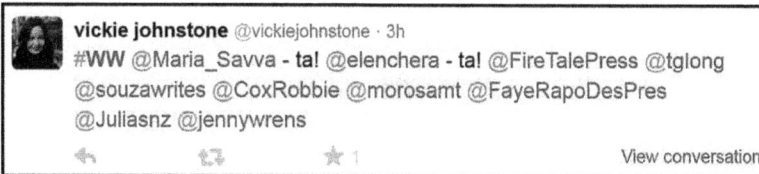

> **vickie johnstone** @vickiejohnstone · 3h
> #WW @Maria_Savva - **ta!** @elenchera - **ta!** @FireTalePress @tglong
> @souzawrites @CoxRobbie @morosamt @FayeRapoDesPres
> @Juliasnz @jennywrens
>
> ↩   ⇋   ★ 1   View conversation

What Vickie's doing here is telling all her followers that these people are worth watching, or following. She's also thanking @Maria_Savva and @elenchera. My guess is she's thanking them for putting Vickie in a #WW tweet.

When someone adds me to a tweet like this, @Urban_Hunters, I get an email from Twitter telling me that I was mentioned in a tweet. The courteous thing for me to do would be to send back a tweet thanking them for the mention, as has happened with the following:

Kassie Kay, or @esldrummer, her username, has sent out a #FF and has had three very appreciative thank yous.

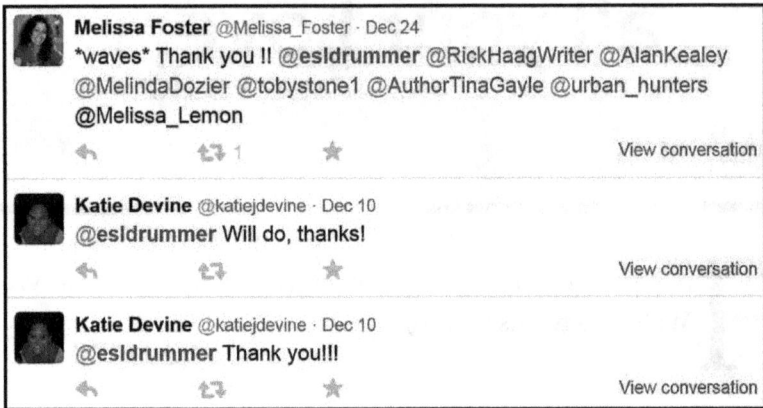

> **Kassie Kay** @esldrummer · May 24
> #FF Favorite #writers on Twitter
> @LornaSuzuki @joycetstrand
> @Rebecca_Forster @NestExpressed
> @AuthorTinaGayle @urban_hunters
> @Melissa_Foster
> ↩ ⟲ 3 ★ 2 •••

> **Melissa Foster** @Melissa_Foster · Dec 24
> *waves* Thank you !! @esldrummer @RickHaagWriter @AlanKealey @MelindaDozier @tobystone1 @AuthorTinaGayle @urban_hunters @Melissa_Lemon
> ↩ ⟲ 1 ★ View conversation

> **Katie Devine** @katiejdevine · Dec 10
> @esldrummer Will do, thanks!
> ↩ ⟲ ★ View conversation

> **Katie Devine** @katiejdevine · Dec 10
> @esldrummer Thank you!!!
> ↩ ⟲ ★ View conversation

Lorna has taken the opportunity to advertise her blog to @esldrummer's followers while thanking her. Mind you, she's missed an opportunity by not including the actual link to her blog.

> **Lorna Suzuki** @LornaSuzuki · May 24 · ••• More
> @esldrummer You're welcome! So many to choose from! I have a blog, too! All Kinds of Writing where I feature indie & trad. published authors
> ↩ ⟲ ★ View conversation

Melissa has done a great job in her thank you by including many of Kassie's #FF list. Kassie will like that, and so will all the people mentioned in Kassie's original #FF list, for which I was included. So now all of Melissa's followers will see that list and possibly drop on over to check out the people in that list. Word–of–mouth in action.

HOW TO DEAL WITH ALL YOUR LOVERS

I've never met or spoken to either of these nice ladies but I would love to thank them for mentioning me. Kassie mentioned me because I'm one of her favourite writers on Twitter and she wants to recommend me to her followers, "Favourite #writers on Twitter", and Melissa mentioned me simply as a favour to Kassie, and for some interesting news for her own followers, telling them about these people who are worth following.

To delve a little deeper into how word–of–mouth is working here, if you have a look at the bottom of Kassie's tweet, you'll see that it has been retweeted three times and favourited twice. Word–of–mouth goes on and on like this and is why it becomes so important to make your advertising tweets entertaining.

Now, back to me thanking them. The dilemma for me is I get quite a few mentions and I don't have the time to reply to them all. Imagine how many retweets with mentions I get with my Amazon Book Page getting 300 to 500 hits everyday. However, thanking people is the right thing to do and it will get me mentioned again so I wondered if I could apply the same hashtag principles to people's usernames. Light bulb moment! Of course I could and my goodness, how fantastically well it would work.

In Kassie's tweet, she had to laboriously type in each and every username into that tweet, and she'll have to do it again the next time, but slightly differently or Twitter won't let her tweet it again. Remember, Twitter won't let you send out the same tweet twice. But what if she was able to group the usernames just like I do with the hashtags? She could run them through my Unlimited Tweet Generator and then set them on AutoPilot through TweetAdder. Bam! She could create hundreds of #FF and #WW and put them all on AutoPilot, generating hundreds of thank yous and retweets without doing one single thing after setting them all up.

[#FF] [@username1|@username2] [@username3|@username4]
[@username5|@username6] [@username7|@username8]
[@username9|@username10] [@username11|@username12]
[@username13|@username14] [@username15|@username16]
[@username17|@username18] [@username19|@username20]
[@username21|@username22]

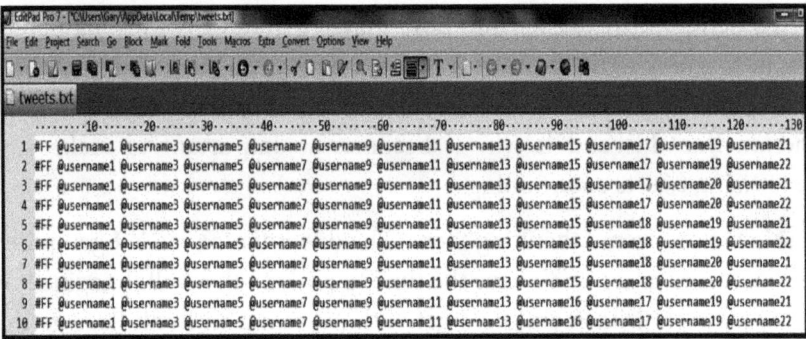

This is what you could do from a thank you perspective:

[#ThankYou] [@username1|@username2] [@username3|@username4]
[@username5|@username6] [@username7|@username8]
[@username9|@username10] [@username11|@username12]
[@username13|@username14] [@username15|@username16]
[@username17|@username18] [@username19|@username20]
[@username21|@username22]

That's a lot of good people thanked on a regular basis without you losing a single second of your writing time. Gotta love that, and no one will ever know that you're doing this on AutoPilot. You've gone to the trouble of thanking them and that's all that matters to them. They'll be so proud of your thank you that they'll retweet it in a heartbeat. Everyone wins. Everyone is happy. Including Twitter who say that if all of your tweets contain links, then that's spamming. This means you're doing the right thing by Twitter and you're getting great mileage out of those tweets.

How to Deal with all your Lovers

The #FF and #ThankYou examples with that many hashtags in those hashtag groups will generate over 2,000 tweets, which is obviously too many. I deleted all but the first 10 tweets in the list, which are mostly odd numbered usernames, and the last 10 tweets, which are mostly even numbered usernames, to give me a selection of 20 username groups that covers everyone. Add or delete from your main lovers list to suit your needs. I wouldn't want more than one of these types of tweets going out in a week.

Another 100,000 Tweets with Just One Click

From time to time you'll have to redo your tweet list. Reasons being:

• You've already used most of the tweets in your list and you need to add a space or a full stop or something to make them different.

• You've found you're spamming a hashtag or username and you have to make changes.

• You've brought out a new book with all new quotes and New Release info so you have to add those and remove the old New Release info.

- You've discovered a new hashtag or username that you want to add, or remove one that isn't working for you.

- You're experimenting.

- Plus a myriad of other reasons.

It can seem daunting with a list of 100,000 tweets but even though I've fine-tuned my list down to 60,000, making changes is pretty simple with the system I set up for doing it.

I make any changes through my main .txt file containing my list of 60,000 tweets, which I run through my EditPad text editing program.

NOTE: That's also the program I use for formatting eBooks. I bought the professional version and haven't looked back.

So I might use the find and replace function within EditPad to make the changes to the entire list. I'll add a space or a full stop or a comma or something like that to each one. Or I might remove all of my old New Release tweets for example, paste them into another .txt file, edit them there and then copy and paste them back into my main .txt file later.

Once I've made all the changes that I need to, I go back into TweetAdder, clear my whole list of tweets, import the new list, randomize them again and that's it, job done.

It really is worth monitoring and experimenting with your hashtags and messages to get the most out of Stampede.

Hashtag Etiquette

I've placed hints and tips on hashtag etiquette throughout these chapters but I thought you'd appreciate some of the more pertinent points gathered in the one place.

- Format your tweets like this: message, link, hashtag sentence.

- Don't try to use hashtags as part of your text message. It looks awful, it's hard to read and it makes it hard to see your link.

- Capitalise keywords in your message e.g.: If you KICK YOUR TOE ON A ROCK, hop around till it feels better. DON'T KICK YOUR OTHER TOE **http://getbook.at/FSSe** #Sage #Advice #lol #YA #HarryPotter

- Don't use more hashtags than you need to just like you wouldn't put unnecessary words into a sentence.

- Make sure you do a thorough check to ensure you're not spamming hashtags.

- Include tweets with no links to give back to the Twitter community and so Twitter doesn't consider you a spammer.

- If someone retweets your tweets, it's polite to thank them but you can take it a step further by going into their profile and retweeting some of their great tweets. They'll be so grateful that they'll come back and retweet some more of your tweets.

Stampede
in a Nutshell

- Create your BookLinker links.

- Create you Twitter account.

- List your tweets from book quotes, testimonials, news, blurbs, hints and tips and promotions like free eBooks.

- Capitalise key words within your quotes etc.

- Gather a list of hashtags relevant to your book along with popularity and usage details. Organise them into subjects like readers and writers for example and put the highest value hashtags according to popularity and usage at the top of each subject group.

- Begin to construct your first tweet using a quote, your link and your selection of hashtags relevant to this tweet. Don't forget to insert your brackets and hashtag separators in preparation of running them through my Tweet Generator.

- Run your first tweet through my Tweet Generator and scan through the tweets generated to see if your hashtags are creating good hashtag sentences.

- If your hashtag groups are not creating good hashtag sentences, go back and make changes to your hashtag groups until you do get good sentences.

- Once you're happy with your hashtag sentences, transfer them to your text editor to see how many tweets are being generated, how long they are from a 140 character count perspective and estimate how many tweets you'll end up with if you remove the tweets that have more than 140 characters. Go back and add or remove hashtags as you need to and run them through my Tweet Generator again until you're satisfied.

- Now move on to your next quote. Don't save your last lot of tweets generated yet because by the time you get to the end of this whole process with all your quotes etc, you may learn something that makes you want to go back and make changes to your first tweets. For example, you may find that you've used a particular hashtag in each and every tweet, which is too often so you have to go back and exchange some of them for another hashtag. And then you may have to check the changed tweets by running them through my Tweet Generator yet again.

- When you've gone through your entire list of quotes etc, do a hashtag count to make sure you haven't used a hashtag too often.

- Now gather all of your generated tweets into one main .txt file.

- Select an AutoPilot program and import your .txt file into it. Randomize your tweets within the program if it allows you to. Set the settings to send out 1 tweet every hour, 24 hours per day in random order.

- 24 hours later, go into Twitter and check your tweets to see if you've made any mistakes, like leaving the actual hashtag symbol off some words and silly things like that. At the same time, do a search in Twitter of every single hashtag that you have used to see if you're spamming those hashtags. If you are, or if you have mistakes to fix, make those changes to as many tweets and hashtags as you need to and then reimport your list back into your AutoPilot program and set it on AutoPilot again.

- 24 hours later, do your spam check again and make changes yet again if you have to.

- Create #ThankYou and #WW tweets, add them to your main tweet.txt file and reimport it to your AutoPilot program.

- Go into BookLinker to see how many hits your Amazon Book Pages have been getting.

- Go to KDP and see how many sales you've been getting.

- While you're kicking back with nothing to do other than count your royalties, duck into Amazon and download some of my Urban Hunters books ;)

Stampede WorkSheet

Create your BookLinker links:

http://getbook.at/............

http://getbook.at/............

Create a selection of Twitter usernames in the hope that you'll be able to use one of them:

@..

@..

@..

STAMPEDE WORKSHEET

List your quotes:

....

....

....

....

....

....

....

....

List your testimonials:

....

....

....

....

....

....

....

....

List your news:

....

....

....

List your blurbs:

....

....

....

....

....

....

....

....

List your hints and tips:

....

....

....

....

....

....

....

....

List your promotions:

....

....

....

STAMPEDE WORKSHEET

Gather relevant hashtags:

#............................. Popularity.......... Usage..........

#.............................P.......... U..........

#.............................P.......... U..........

#.............................P........ U..........

#.............................P.......... U..........

#.............................P.......... U..........

#.............................P.......... U..........

#.............................P.......... U..........

#.............................P.......... U..........

#.............................P.......... U..........

#.............................P.......... U..........

#.............................P.......... U..........

#.............................P.......... U..........

#.............................P.......... U..........

#.............................P.......... U..........

Construct your tweets:

[Your quote... http://getbook.at/.....]
[#..............................|#..................................|#.............................]
[#..............................|#..................................|#.............................]
[#..............................|#..................................|#.............................]
[#..............................|#..................................|#.............................]
[#..............................|#..................................|#.............................]
[#..............................|#..................................|#.............................]

[Your quote.. http://getbook.at/.....]
[#....................................|#....................................|#....................................]
[#....................................|#....................................|#....................................]
[#....................................|#....................................|#....................................]
[#....................................|#....................................|#....................................]
[#....................................|#....................................|#....................................]
[#....................................|#....................................|#....................................]

[Your quote.. http://getbook.at/.....]
[#....................................|#....................................|#....................................]
[#....................................|#....................................|#....................................]
[#....................................|#....................................|#....................................]
[#....................................|#....................................|#....................................]
[#....................................|#....................................|#....................................]
[#....................................|#....................................|#....................................]

[Your quote.. http://getbook.at/.....]
[#....................................|#....................................|#....................................]
[#....................................|#....................................|#....................................]
[#....................................|#....................................|#....................................]
[#....................................|#....................................|#....................................]
[#....................................|#....................................|#....................................]
[#....................................|#....................................|#....................................]

[Your quote.. http://getbook.at/.....]
[#....................................|#....................................|#....................................]
[#....................................|#....................................|#....................................]
[#....................................|#....................................|#....................................]
[#....................................|#....................................|#....................................]
[#....................................|#....................................|#....................................]
[#....................................|#....................................|#....................................]

STAMPEDE WORKSHEET

[Your quote.. http://getbook.at/.....]
[#.................................|#.................................|#.................................]
[#.................................|#.................................|#.................................]
[#.................................|#.................................|#.................................]
[#.................................|#.................................|#.................................]
[#.................................|#.................................|#.................................]
[#.................................|#.................................|#.................................]

[Your quote.. http://getbook.at/.....]
[#.................................|#.................................|#.................................]
[#.................................|#.................................|#.................................]
[#.................................|#.................................|#.................................]
[#.................................|#.................................|#.................................]
[#.................................|#.................................|#.................................]
[#.................................|#.................................|#.................................]

[Your quote.. http://getbook.at/.....]
[#.................................|#.................................|#.................................]
[#.................................|#.................................|#.................................]
[#.................................|#.................................|#.................................]
[#.................................|#.................................|#.................................]
[#.................................|#.................................|#.................................]
[#.................................|#.................................|#.................................]

[Your quote.. http://getbook.at/.....]
[#.................................|#.................................|#.................................]
[#.................................|#.................................|#.................................]
[#.................................|#.................................|#.................................]
[#.................................|#.................................|#.................................]
[#.................................|#.................................|#.................................]
[#.................................|#.................................|#.................................]

[Your quote.. http://getbook.at/.....]
[#.............................|#.............................|#.............................]
[#.............................|#.............................|#.............................]
[#.............................|#.............................|#.............................]
[#.............................|#.............................|#.............................]
[#.............................|#.............................|#.............................]
[#.............................|#.............................|#.............................]

[Your quote.. http://getbook.at/.....]
[#.............................|#.............................|#.............................]
[#.............................|#.............................|#.............................]
[#.............................|#.............................|#.............................]
[#.............................|#.............................|#.............................]
[#.............................|#.............................|#.............................]
[#.............................|#.............................|#.............................]

[Your quote.. http://getbook.at/.....]
[#.............................|#.............................|#.............................]
[#.............................|#.............................|#.............................]
[#.............................|#.............................|#.............................]
[#.............................|#.............................|#.............................]
[#.............................|#.............................|#.............................]
[#.............................|#.............................|#.............................]

[Your quote.. http://getbook.at/.....]
[#.............................|#.............................|#.............................]
[#.............................|#.............................|#.............................]
[#.............................|#.............................|#.............................]
[#.............................|#.............................|#.............................]
[#.............................|#.............................|#.............................]
[#.............................|#.............................|#.............................]

STAMPEDE WORKSHEET

[Your quote.. http://getbook.at/.....]
[#....................................|#....................................|#....................................]
[#....................................|#....................................|#....................................]
[#....................................|#....................................|#....................................]
[#....................................|#....................................|#....................................]
[#....................................|#....................................|#....................................]
[#....................................|#....................................|#....................................]

[Your quote.. http://getbook.at/.....]
[#....................................|#....................................|#....................................]
[#....................................|#....................................|#....................................]
[#....................................|#....................................|#....................................]
[#....................................|#....................................|#....................................]
[#....................................|#....................................|#....................................]
[#....................................|#....................................|#....................................]

[Your quote.. http://getbook.at/.....]
[#....................................|#....................................|#....................................]
[#....................................|#....................................|#....................................]
[#....................................|#....................................|#....................................]
[#....................................|#....................................|#....................................]
[#....................................|#....................................|#....................................]
[#....................................|#....................................|#....................................]

Construct your #ThankYou and #WW tweets:

[#ThankYou] [@........................|@........................|@........................]
[@........................|@........................|@........................]
[@........................|@........................|@........................]
[@........................|@........................|@........................]
[@........................|@........................|@........................]

[@.....................|@......................|@..........................]
[@.....................|@......................|@..........................]

[#ThankYou] [@.....................|@...................|@....................]
[@.....................|@......................|@..........................]
[@.....................|@......................|@..........................]
[@.....................|@......................|@..........................]
[@.....................|@......................|@..........................]
[@.....................|@......................|@..........................]
[@.....................|@......................|@..........................]

[#WW] [@.........................|@..................|@..........................]
[@.....................|@......................|@..........................]
[@.....................|@......................|@..........................]
[@.....................|@......................|@..........................]
[@.....................|@......................|@..........................]
[@.....................|@......................|@..........................]
[@.....................|@......................|@..........................]

[#WW] [@.........................|@..................|@..........................]
[@.....................|@......................|@..........................]
[@.....................|@......................|@..........................]
[@.....................|@......................|@..........................]
[@.....................|@......................|@..........................]
[@.....................|@......................|@..........................]
[@.....................|@......................|@..........................]

Prepare a spreadsheet to count your royalties:

$$$

Conclusion

I've seen lots of clever advances in marketing but I've never seen anything as spectacularly successful as this. It really is a giant leap forward and I'm really excited for you. Please spread the word and tell others about this great system— Stampede works!

BUNYA
PUBLISHING.com

Thank You!

Thank you for reading Stampede. I really do hope you enjoyed it and more than that, I hope you achieve lots of great successes with my system.

I'd really love to hear from you. I'd love to know how you've gone implementing my system and how well it has worked for you. Did you learn any handy hints and tips and tricks along the way that you'd like to share with others? Share them with me and I'll add them to updated versions of this book.

I'll be bringing out more How To books so if you'd like to be among the first to hear of new releases, please subscribe to my **Newsletter**. At the same time, if there's a particular type of How To book that you'd like me to write then please feel free to let me know via **email**. You know it's going to be a no nonsense guidebook that cuts straight through the usual hyped up nonsense.

Would you like to help me create a BUZZ about Stampede or my Urban Hunters series? Please head on over to **BunyaPublishing.com** and hit the **Buzz** link to find out how you can help. Thanks heaps for your support.

Good luck with all your endeavours and see you next time …

About the Author

Gary's been selling products direct to consumers for over a quarter of a century. All the way back to when the fax machine was the latest and greatest and was used more often than email. He was there when Netscape, the first popular internet browser gave everyone easy access to the internet and watched in wonder as MySpace and Facebook connected friends and consumers all over the world.

He's used snail mail, fax mail, email and now Stampede, his most successful marketing strategy ever. Many times more successful than anything he's ever developed. To say he's excited about it would have to be the understatement of the century.

He's travelled the world, invented security products for Harley-Davidson and self-published eight books for the Young Adult market. Of all the things he's done, marketing is what he does best and that's what this book is all about. And it's just the beginning. He has lots more up his sleeve so stay tuned for more outstanding products from this savvy marketer.

Connect with Gary here:

NEWSLETTER...http://eepurl.com/TFWkf
Twitter ....@Urban_Hunters
Facebook Author Page ....Gary   Taaffe
Email ....gmt369@gmail.com
Bookstore & TWEET GENERATORS........www.BunyaPublishing.com
Blog...www.UrbanHunters.com.au

Want to Read Something Funny?

I f you want to read Twilight clones or Fifty Shades of Grey clones or any of the other clones out there then my Urban Hunters series is definitely not for you. But if you want to read something completely different, then I invite you to give my Urban Hunters series a go. I've never heard anyone say they didn't love the series, young or old, so if you want a laugh and want to be taken to a completely different world, then drop on in for an Urban Hunters adventure.

I have 12 books planned in the series with 8 out so far. You can download the first one for free here: **http://bit.ly/11ZMOtt**

Or if you'd prefer, head straight on over to Amazon: **http://getbook.at/FSSe**

www.ingramcontent.com/pod-product-compliance
Lightning Source LLC
Chambersburg PA
CBHW060624210326
41520CB00010B/1460